Habits That Heal

A Spiritual Journey to Physical Wellness

LINDA BASTIAN BARNEY

BALBOA.
PRESS

A DIVISION OF HAY HOUSE

Balboa Press books may be ordered through booksellers or by contacting:

Balboa Press
A Division of Hay House
1663 Liberty Drive
Bloomington, IN 47403
www.balboapress.com
1 (877) 407-4847

Because of the dynamic nature of the Internet, any web addresses or
links contained in this book may have changed since publication and
may no longer be valid. The views expressed in this work are solely those
of the author and do not necessarily reflect the views of the publisher,
and the publisher hereby disclaims any responsibility for them.

The author of this book does not dispense medical advice or prescribe
the use of any technique as a form of treatment for physical, emotional,
or medical problems without the advice of a physician, either directly
or indirectly. The intent of the author is only to offer information
of a general nature to help you in your quest for emotional and
spiritual well-being. In the event you use any of the information in
this book for yourself, which is your constitutional right, the author
and the publisher assume no responsibility for your actions.

Any people depicted in stock imagery provided by Thinkstock are
models, and such images are being used for illustrative purposes only.
Certain stock imagery © Thinkstock.

Printed in the United States of America.

ISBN: 978-1-4525-2216-6 (sc)
ISBN: 978-1-4525-2217-3 (e)

Balboa Press rev. date: 09/19/2014

For My Family:

I hope I always make you proud.

Contents

Foreword

I have known Linda and watched her story as her neighbor and chiropractor since she was a young mother and wife with one child. I have watched and seen the transformation of her life and attitude. She has truly lived her own personal "journey to wellness," and has been relentless in searching for truth and wellness principles that work.

She has given you a gift by writing her story and being honest about the process so that you can relate to her story and see your way to wellness. If you will read and apply these habits for healing, you will transform your life and find joy and peace in your wellness journey.

Linda has shown us the way and now it is your choice: Stay stuck in your 'stuff' or look up and live well with gratitude and love!

Are you ready? Then read and apply. It is guaranteed to change your life!

Dr. Randall Roberts DC
Director of Soli Wellness Center

Author's Note

I have always wanted to write a book. Ever since I can remember it was a dream of mine. I think it began because of my grandmother. She was a gifted writer who penned poetry, short stories, biographies and histories. She also wrote comedy sketches that she and her best friend would perform for church activities and at the local retirement home.

I can still see her sitting at the table in her sunny yellow kitchen with a pen and spiral bound notepad and just writing for hours. She would produce eloquent, beautiful poems and stories that made you laugh and cry and think. I wanted to do that too. I felt like I had a small part of her gift, and I hoped that someday I could be a writer like her.

My grandma wasn't a published author, but I don't think that ever mattered to her. She wrote because she loved it, because it meant something to her, and it touched people's hearts. People loved reading her stories and frequently asked her to write things for them, so in a way, she was famous. Everyone that knew her knew she was a writer. It was her identity.

My writing "career" was not quite as stellar as my grandmother's. I wrote poems and short stories as a teenager and I was on the journalism staff in high school. I got a little bit of attention for being a writer from time to time, and had a few teachers tell me I should pursue a writing career. With that small bit of encouragement, I went off to college determined to major in journalism.

It didn't take long for me to realize that being a news writer just wasn't for me. I didn't have the thick skin that journalists need in order to survive. The first time I tried to interview someone and was yelled at for it, I cried. So I picked another major, one that didn't require me to be so "out there" and forgot about being a writer. Except, I didn't forget.

Over all the years of my life while raising my children, working, and living day-to-day, the dream was still there in the back of my mind. I wanted to be an author. I wanted to write a book. I didn't know what I would write about, I just knew I needed to do it, but I didn't know how. And if I did manage to write a book, who would read it? It was a huge, scary, intimidating prospect, so I waited. And waited.

Now, at the age of forty-seven, I am finally doing it. And honestly, if no one but my closest family and friends ever read it, that's okay with me. This is just something I have to do, and so I am doing it. Maybe I will even receive some inspiration from a gifted writer that I once knew. I feel that she is guiding me in this endeavor, and I hope that I make her proud.

My grandma didn't change the world with her writing, but she changed mine. She made me see that I could be creative, smart, intellectual, funny, honest, sad, and everything else and just let it spill out onto the paper. I could be more real and alive by being a writer than I could any other way.

This is my book. This is the truth of me. I hope you find something in here that helps you love and appreciate your body, your mind, your heart, and your soul. I hope that by telling you my truth and my story, it helps you on your journey in some way. This is my journey to wellness, but it is also my journey to me, and to really learning to love myself. It is about God, and His great love for each of us. It is about the connection we have to Him, and about His willingness to help us in every single aspect of our lives— even in our quest for physical health.

It is my intention to help you see how wonderful and magnificent you are. You are a child of a great Creator. He gave you an amazing body to house your mind and spirit and He expects you to care for it in the most exceptional way. I think He wants you to remember Him as you care for this physical body, this temporary dwelling place of your spirit while you journey here on earth. And I also believe that He will help you to know how to care for it, love it, honor it, and feed it so that it can do it's very best to work for you.

We are only given one body. We don't get handed another one if we wear this one out, abuse it, or neglect it. The body you inhabit is an amazing gift from someone who loves you more than you can imagine. He gave you the exact body you would need in order to learn the lessons you needed to learn from it. Every single thing about this body—the curves of your face, the length of your bones, the color of your eyes, the texture of your skin—is unique only to you. This body was created just for you to dwell in, experience life in, work in, and serve others in until the day you die and you give it back to God.

It is up to you to take extremely good care of this gift—your physical body, this wonderful vessel you were given. This is a huge responsibility, or even a stewardship if you want to call it that. It can be difficult to know the best things to do—what foods to take in, what foods to avoid, how much rest to get, and how often to exercise. But, you don't have to do it all alone.

Who cares about your body even more than you do? Probably only one person—the One who created it. It makes sense, at least to me, that the Creator of your body would know exactly how to instruct you to care for the body that He gave you. He has told us we can turn to Him for help in all things, so why not ask for His help in caring for our physical health?

This book is a guide to developing the habits that will aid us in caring for our physical bodies in the most spiritual ways possible. All things are created spiritually before they are created physically, and the same is true for our bodies. It is our job to do the spiritual work of envisioning and bringing into existence the vibrant, energetic, healthy bodies we crave under the direction of the One who created them and us.

Introduction

My story, as it pertains to this book, begins in the middle. Well, sort of. It begins in the middle-ish area of my life. I was a full-time mother of three young boys that I absolutely adored. I was busy, I was stressed out, and I was pretty unhealthy. The truth of it is, I felt like crap. I could not seem to find the energy and joy for life that I had once had. I felt completely out of balance. I did not have any major health issues, for which I was and am grateful, but I had what I can only describe as a general feeling of un-wellness. I had lost my zest for life. My "sparkle" was gone.

I was not overweight, not underweight, just average size. I was blessed with a small frame and never had a problem with my weight, for which I am grateful. But even though my weight was normal, I didn't feel "normal." I was tired most of the time. My joints, muscles, and head ached almost constantly. I experienced bouts of depression as well as a constant feeling of anxiety and frequent panic attacks in the middle of the night. I took Benadryl in order to sleep at night, and I drank caffeine and ate chocolate during the day to perk myself up. I was taking eight to ten over-the-counter pain relievers a day for my aching head and body. I guess I must have believed that my body was deficient in sugar, caffeine, and pain relievers, because I used them excessively to try and feel better! I was doing what a lot, if not most mothers do—I was putting my children, my husband, and everyone else first, and taking care of myself last.

My "crisis/awakening" occurred around the time of my thirtieth birthday. Going from being in your twenties to being in your thirties is kind of a big deal, a major shift in life for most people. But for me it was absolutely terrifying. I was scared to death of the fact that my thirty-year-old body felt more like it was fifty. I thought, if I feel run-down, depressed and lethargic at age thirty, how will I feel when I turn forty, or fifty, or sixty? I could not imagine living life feeling old, tired and sick all the time. I wanted to feel vibrant, healthy, strong, and alive. I wanted to see my kids grow up, get married, and have families of their own. My oldest son, Michael, had dreams of becoming a doctor when he grew up, and I couldn't help but envision him a few years down the road, having to care for his sick, old mother and make sure she took her medicine.

I knew I had to make some major changes in my life, and I had to start right away. I had no idea what exactly I needed to do or how I would do it, but I made a commitment to myself that I would do whatever it took to get myself well.

The first thing that occurred to me was to change the food I was eating. I knew instinctively that eating packaged, chemically enhanced foods filled with preservatives was not doing me or my family any good. I knew I needed to make better choices in the foods I ate and the meals I prepared for my family. I also knew all the stimulants and painkillers I had been taking were part of why I felt so sick, even though doctors didn't seem too concerned when I mentioned it to them. I felt that "going natural" was going to be the way I would get well. I also knew that it was going to take time and patience.

I started by buying wheat bread that looked and tasted like white bread. I switched to frozen vegetables instead of canned. I visited the farmers' market and challenged myself to buy vegetables I had never tried before. At first, my family wasn't happy. They liked the old, fluffy white bread we used to eat. They loved eating cold sugared cereal for breakfast every morning. That's the thing about processed foods—they are addicting. We learned this when we started trying to wean ourselves off them. There was a little complaining and a lot of trial and error, but I persevered. I was determined I was going to get healthy, and I was going to drag my family along with me kicking and screaming. Since I was the one who did the majority of the shopping and cooking, they didn't really have a choice.

The more I studied, read and learned, the more changes I made. I began including more whole grains in our family's diet, and eventually we were eating whole wheat bread, fresh vegetables, and even having "exotic" side dishes with dinner like quinoa and brown rice. We reduced the amount of meat we ate, and started having "Meatless Mondays". We made an effort to eat locally grown foods whenever we could and grew our own vegetables in our back yard. We didn't eat perfectly all of the time, but we were doing better and making progress. We could all feel it.

I will be the first to admit that for the first little while, it was really hard. I missed eating candy whenever I wanted, and making quick and easy dinners of frozen chicken nuggets and boxed mac & cheese. But, after a few months, I realized something; I was feeling much better, so I kept going. I kept learning, studying and researching. I kept making small changes to the way I ate and fed my family, and we lived through it! In fact, we started thriving! My youngest son, who had been so addicted to cold sugared cereals that he had to have it three times a day, was now asking me to make him a healthy breakfast every morning. It took a little more time to make a fresh homemade smoothie and some bran toast than it did to pour a bowl of cold cereal, but I didn't mind. I was so happy he was actually craving food that was good for him, that I was happy to do it.

In 2011, as part of my commitment to learning all I could about nutrition, I enrolled in a health-coaching program with the Institute of Integrative Nutrition and became a certified holistic health coach. I wanted to be able to teach others the importance of natural healing and a holistic approach to wellness. It was this yearlong course that began to transform the way I looked at the health of my body, mind and spirit. I could no longer view my physical health as being separate from my mental and spiritual health. My training taught me that they are inseparable and intertwined in ways I had never imagined.

* * *

The process of going from mindlessly eating whatever was cheap and easy-to-prepare to carefully choosing and preparing healthy, nutritious foods led me to another interesting revelation; I was really, *really* thankful for my body. I began to view my body as a precious gift, and I was learning to love and appreciate this gift as I never had before.

I began to listen to my body, trust its intuition and instincts, and to truly respect it for the magnificent creation that it is. Even though it is not perfect, this body is mine. It was created specifically for me—for my learning experiences and growth while here on earth. It is an incredible gift given to me by my loving Father and now I was finally giving it the care and attention that it deserved.

The cool thing I discovered about loving your body is that once you start to really love and appreciate it, it starts loving you back! That may sound a little crazy, but think about it this way. How do we respond when someone treats us unkindly, abuses us or neglects us? We don't spend much time or effort trying to love them and take care of them, do we? It is the same with our bodies. As we grow to truly care for and lovingly nurture our bodies, they respond by giving love back to us in the form of health, energy, and vitality.

The more I loved and appreciated my body, the more I also loved and appreciated others. I think it is a law of nature that when you feel good about yourself, you automatically feel good about the people around you. I had an increased desire to serve and support my family, friends, and neighbors and even people I didn't know. I wanted to show love to everyone as often as possible!

* * *

Besides making changes in the way I ate, cooked, and felt about my body, I also began to make changes in my daily habits and routine. Where once I had sporadically read scriptures and other uplifting books, and written in my journal from time to time, I began to set aside an hour every morning for gratitude, journaling, meditation, and spiritual study. I had no idea at the time that this would affect my health, but I later learned that it was crucial to my mental, emotional, and physical well-being.

I began to pray for help and guidance to know how to help my body heal itself, and I also began asking for help in *wanting* to do healthy things like exercise and eat nutritiously. I began to recognize the importance of love, learning, gratitude, stillness, prayer, peacefulness, and service as they pertained to my own physical health and wellness. These things, I later learned, were just as important, if not more important, than the foods that I ate or the amount of exercise I got.

Keep in mind that the changes I made were instinctive. I was acting on what I call spiritual promptings. I believe that God communicates to each of us through his Spirit. He is able to instruct us through feelings, thoughts, and messages in our bodies. I made a conscious effort to listen for and follow those promptings when I received them.

Nobody was telling me what books to read or how much to meditate. Nobody was instructing me on what acts of kindness to perform or how many times a day I should pray. But people, I like to call them teachers, did begin to show up in my life. At the very times I needed to learn a certain way of being or doing things, someone would show up in my life and teach me, through their actions or through the things they talked about, the very thing I needed to learn at that time. I began to be on the lookout for those who would be coming to show me the way. I truly learned to believe in the saying, "When the student is ready, the teacher will appear."

There were other "teachers" that showed up as well. These teachers were life experiences. I had many difficult, painful, joyful, scary, wonderful learning experiences along the way that taught me about who I was, who I needed to become, and what I needed to do in order to grow, learn, and transform. This is a journey we all take—there is no way to escape the life lessons that God has in store for us. The trick is to recognize them for what they are, embrace them, and let them make us whole.

In this book, I have organized the thoughts, feelings, and lessons I have learned in the hopes that it may help some other fellow searcher find their way to health, happiness, and healing. It is my fondest wish that you will find some truth in what I have to share, and that it will guide or inspire you on your own personal journey to wellness.

Habit #1: Gratitude

"And let the peace of God rule in your hearts, to the which also ye are called in one body; and be ye thankful." Colossians 3:15 (King James Version)

Be thankful for Your Body

For years and years, I hated my body. I didn't spend much time thinking about all the great things my body was doing for me; I only thought about all the things I thought were wrong with it. I realize that I am not the only person who ever felt this way. In fact, I think most of us have something about our bodies that we wish we could change. But at the time, it seemed like everyone but me was totally fine with who they were and were totally comfortable in their own skin. In my mind, I was the only one who had a problem.

When I was a kid, I didn't think about my body at all. Man, those were great times! I just ran and played and jumped and had fun, and my body took me where I needed to go. I ate when my body was hungry, and I slept when it got tired. When it got sick, I rested, and when it felt good, I took it all over the place from sunup to sundown. We got along great back then, my body and I.

As I grew up and became a teenager, I started to realize that my body was not like most of my friends. That's when the hatred began. I hated my arms and legs. I was extremely thin and lanky and awkward looking. I guess you could say I was all elbows and knees—skinny limbs and big, knobby-looking joints. I also had thick, black hair all over my arms. I hated that too. One particularly cruel classmate thought it was great fun to call me "Monkey Arms," which didn't do much for my self-esteem.

I hated my pale skin. I would spend hours baking my skin in the sun, slathering on baby oil spiked with iodine, trying to get my fair, British hide to turn golden brown. But mostly it would just burn, peel, and turn back to a pasty white again. I hated my teeth. I felt that they were way too big for my face and made me look cartoonish and weird, like Bugs Bunny. I hated my nose too. I thought the bridge was entirely too wide and out of proportion with the rest of my face. I longed for a dainty, little, slim nose instead.

I hated my hair. In the eighties, everyone had poufy, curly hair, and mine was straight as a stick. I spent countless hours perming, blow-drying, curling and basically frying the crap out of my hair to get it to look like everyone else's. Mostly I just wanted to fit in, to be like everybody else and not stand out. But my body was not cooperating.

There was pretty much only one thing I liked about my body—my green eyes. That was it. During those teenage years, they were all I could really find about myself that I could appreciate. It makes me so sad now to look back on all those years of hating my body and realize that I felt little, if any, gratitude for this magnificent gift I had been given.

Even after I became an adult, got married, and had a family, the hatred continued. I hated my stomach because, after having three children, it was not as firm or as flat as it had once been. I still hated my hair and continued to try to abuse it into doing what I wanted it to do. I still hated my skin, too, and had resorted to visiting tanning salons two to three times a week so I could look more tan and "healthy." I had gotten braces as an adult and had sort of "grown into" my giant teeth, so that hatred had somewhat subsided, but there were still many things about myself that didn't meet my approval and that I could beat myself up for.

I wasted a lot of time hating myself, wishing that my body, or at least parts of it, could be anything but what it was. No wonder by the time I hit age thirty my body had given up on me. I had given up on it long ago, and it literally couldn't take it anymore. Just like anyone or anything else that is neglected, despised, and abused, my body became weak and sick. Really, I'm amazed it didn't happen sooner.

After my age-thirty crisis/awakening, I realized that I had been extremely neglectful, at times abusive, and downright ungrateful for this body I had been given. I began for the first time in my life to really try to love, appreciate, and care for my body. As I said earlier, I started by choosing to eat more nutritious foods, and my body responded by giving me more energy, strength, and vitality. As my body began to heal, I was finally starting to get it: my body was changing because I was giving it love instead of hate. Imagine that!

How do you learn to love something that you have spent so much time and energy hating for years and years on end? Gratitude. You bring gratitude to it. I'm not talking about just a general feeling of, "Oh, I am grateful for my body," or a passing thought now and then, like "Hey, body, you're doing great. Keep up the good work." I am talking about a daily practice, the same way you do other things every day, like brush your teeth, go to the gym, or walk the dog. Gratitude, in order for it to be effective and transformative, has to be practiced daily.

My gratitude practice started out as journaling. I would write down a list of ten things I was grateful for every day. Bringing gratitude to my body instead of constantly finding fault with it was very refreshing. It wasn't always easy to find something about my body that I loved, but it felt much better to focus on what was right with me instead of always trashing myself. Each day, I tried to genuinely feel the gratitude for my body that I had lacked for so many years, and I began to feel a lot different about myself when I looked in the mirror. I soon realized that making a conscious effort to truly be thankful for this body led me to treat it with much more respect and reverence. I also realized that I was feeling better physically. Studies show that people who keep a daily gratitude journal are more optimistic, feel better about life, exercise more, and have fewer visits to physicians than those who do not practice gratitude regularly. They also tend to get more sleep, fall asleep faster, and awaken feeling more refreshed. This was certainly proving to be true in my case.

After I had been gratitude journaling for a while, a friend of mine told me about another way of practicing gratitude. He said that first thing in the morning, as soon as he opened his eyes, he would make a mental list of ten things he was grateful for. The rule was that he couldn't get up until he had listed ten things. I loved the idea of starting off the day with gratitude right from the get-go, so I started doing it. It took some practice because, honestly, my first thought every morning was not "I am grateful"; it was more along the lines of "Crap, I have to get up now." But I persevered, and in time, I was making my mental list every morning before my feet even touched the ground. I tried to think of new things I was grateful for each day so I wasn't repeating myself. That would kind of defeat the purpose, I thought.

When you force yourself to come up with a new list each day, you find a lot of interesting things to be grateful for. Besides the usual things like family, home, and health, some of the more interesting things I found myself feeling thankful for were the ocean, cheese, my dishwasher, lotion, Christmas-scented candles, my lungs, my kitchen cabinets, and warm, fuzzy socks. I realized that the list could go on forever because I had an abundance of things to be grateful for.

Another amazing gratitude practice is to write a letter to your body. I learned this concept during my health-coaching training. I found the idea intriguing, so one day I sat down and wrote to my body, telling it how much I loved it, and how much I appreciated all that it has done for me throughout my life. I told my body that I was sorry for all of the rotten, abusive, and neglectful things I had done to it over the years, but now I knew better and would treat it with much more tenderness and care going forward. I made a list of all the things I would do to show love and gratitude for my body and signed my name at the bottom of the letter. It may sound like a strange thing to do, but I promise you that this powerful exercise helped me develop a deeper sense of love and connection to my wonderful, incredible, miraculous body.

Because of my gratitude practice, I gradually began to see everything, even my body, in a whole new light. Instead of despising certain parts of my body for not being perfect, or not looking a certain way, I felt gratitude for the proper function and overall health of my body and all of its parts. I no longer hated my stomach because it wasn't as flat as I wanted it to be. I loved and appreciated my stomach and my digestive system for taking in the food I ate, breaking it down, and getting out of it all the nutrients it possibly could. Instead of struggling against the natural tendency of my hair, I started being nice to it. I was careful about what products I used and made a conscious effort to be less abusive when I styled it.

Because of my years of sun worshipping and going to tanning beds, I developed basal cell skin cancer lesions on my back, chest, neck, and hands. Hating my appearance had done one thing for me: it kept me from getting skin cancer on my face because I always wore foundation. After having several pre-cancer and cancer lesions surgically removed, I realized how much I loved my skin, and how thankful I was for it. My skin had worked hard my whole life to protect my bones, muscles, and internal organs, and what had I done to thank it? I spent years baking it in the sun, cursing it for not being what I wanted it to be, and hating it for the way it looked. But now, for the first time, I was good to my skin. I thanked it for allowing me to feel, touch, and experience life and for protecting me from the elements. I used natural products and essential oils that helped it to heal, and protected it when I went out in the sun.

Martin Luther King Jr. once said, *"Darkness cannot drive out darkness; only light can do that. Hate cannot drive out hate; only love can do that."* It wasn't easy and it didn't happen overnight, but eventually I no longer hated any part of my body I had once deemed imperfect. Being grateful for my body had actually changed not just my perception of it, but my body itself. Because I loved it, was grateful for it, and treated it well, my body began to be healthy, vibrant, and beautiful. That is the transforming power of love. And love begins with gratitude.

"Have you ever contemplated the wonder of yourself, the eyes with which you see, the ears with which you hear, the voice with which you speak? No camera ever built can compare with the human eye. No method of communication ever devised can compare with the voice or the ear. No pump ever built will run as long or as efficiently as the human heart. What a remarkable creature each of us is! We can think by day and dream by night. We can speak and hear, smell and taste and feel. We can store what we experience and learn in a remarkable retrieval system unmatched by the most spectacular computer. We can learn and grow and progress and become better tomorrow than we are today...

I believe the human body to be the creation of divinity. Our bodies were designed and created by the Almighty to be the tabernacles, the earthly receptacles, of our eternal spirits.

We ought to be grateful for the growing accumulation of knowledge about taking care of the body. The smoking of a single cigarette, actuarially speaking, will result in a loss of seven minutes of life for the smoker. Knowing that is so, how can any thoughtful individual make the deliberate choice to smoke? Or take debilitating drugs into his or her system? Or expose himself or herself to...health risks that result from abuse of the body and total disregard of one's future?"
(Gordon B. Hinckley, Standing for Something, pp. 91-92)

A Lesson In Gratitude

The Worst and Best Day of My Life

No parent is ever prepared to take a phone call like the one my husband and I received on September 19, 2010. We were in church. My son, Jaron, who was attending college at the University of Utah, about 45 minutes from our home, had been texting me that morning. He had been battling depression and anxiety for about a year, and I had been checking in with him to see if he was coming home for dinner that day. He told me that he had taken some meds for his anxiety, so he wasn't sure if he should drive. I told him that I didn't want him driving if he was medicated, and that he should probably stay at his apartment.

Of course, I was worried. I kept thinking about Jaron and the chance that he might try to drive home and possibly get in a car accident. As a mother, you never stop worrying about your children, no matter how old they get. As I sat in Sunday School, I felt as if my chair were electrified, and I wanted to jump up, run out of the room, and call Jaron immediately, but I didn't. I don't know why I didn't.

As soon as Sunday School was over, my husband checked his phone, and there was a voice message from Jaron. He said he was sorry, and that he didn't want us to be mad at him. He had taken all the medication he had in the apartment in an attempt to take his own life. He was being taken to the hospital. That was the end of the message. Jaron later told us it had taken him a few hours to swallow all the pills, and then he had fallen asleep. After sleeping, he didn't know for how long, something, a feeling of being shocked or startled, had awakened him, and he had called 911.

Without even knowing what hospital we were heading for, my husband, my youngest son, Devin, and I jumped into the car and started down the freeway. My head was spinning. This couldn't be happening. I couldn't get my mind to make sense of any of this. I knew that Jaron had been depressed, and he had been in therapy for a year. He had also been on many prescription medications to try and deal with the problem, but diagnosing mental illness is not an exact science. It is a process of trial and error to come up with the right combination and dosages of medications for each individual. He had been on a wide variety of antidepressant, antipsychotic, and antianxiety pills. I was very uncomfortable with him being on such strong medications, but I put my trust in the doctors and in Jaron's ability to decide for himself what the best course of action was.

I remember telling my husband he wasn't driving fast enough. He needed to go faster. I needed to get to my son. I needed to be there for him. I knew they would be pumping his stomach to rid his body of all the poisonous chemicals, and I also knew there was a chance that it would be too late.

There were a few minutes of complete chaos as we tried calling around to different hospitals to see if Jaron had been taken to any of them. I was getting more and more frantic, and I couldn't remember how to work my cell phone. Finally, while driving eighty miles per hour down the freeway, my husband grabbed the phone from me and dialed 911. He was able to find out from the dispatcher that Jaron had been taken to the University of Utah Medical Center.

After what seemed like hours of driving, we finally arrived at the hospital. The receptionist at the emergency room desk said we would have to wait a few minutes before we could see our son. I made a few phone calls to family members to let them know what had happened, and then I collapsed onto the floor of the waiting room. I just crumpled into a heap on the carpet and sobbed. This was beyond anything I had ever had to bear before, and I didn't think I was going to be able to do it. I knew I had to stay strong for my family and for Jaron, but I didn't know how.

At this point, I had let go of any pride that was keeping me calm and composed, and I just let everything out. I didn't care who was watching or what they might think. I was at my breaking point. Nothing mattered except Jaron being okay. He had to make it through this. We all did.

At that moment, I felt an arm around my shoulder. Jaron's best friend from high school, Sadie, had somehow found out what had happened and had come to the hospital. Sadie was like the daughter I never had, and was very close with our whole family. She sat down on the floor with me, wrapped her arms around me, and cried with me. I don't remember her speaking any words of comfort, although she may have said something. I only remember her getting on the floor with me at my lowest moment and being right there with me. It was the kindest thing I think anyone had ever done for me in my entire life.

As I sat there sobbing, my entire body was flooded with anguish and fear as I imagined the worst possible scenarios that we could be facing. What if Jaron didn't make it through this? How would our family ever survive such a horrible loss? What if he survived but had irreparable damage to his brain or body? For a few moments, I allowed my mind to go to the very darkest thoughts that it could conjure up, but then an incredible thing happened. A peaceful feeling came over me, and I was filled with an overwhelming sense of peace, gratitude, and love. I felt God's love for me, for my son, and for all of us. Something within me shifted from despair to hope, and I knew in that moment that Jaron was going to be okay. No matter what happened, everything was going to be okay. I was grateful for this feeling of peace, for my family there supporting me, and for a sweet friend's willingness to go with me into one of the darkest moments of life. Gratitude. I just felt gratitude.

Even though we were told the wait would only be a few minutes, it was ninety minutes before the nurse came out to get me and take me back to see Jaron. She said that only I could come, no other family members. Jaron had assured her that I "liked medical stuff," and I would be able to handle it. I tried to mentally prepare myself for what I might see, and reminded myself not to cry. I had to be strong for Jaron. I couldn't fall apart and make him even more worried or scared than he already was.

I didn't know how my legs were working as I followed the nurse down the hallway and into a little room in the ER. I felt like I was in some crazy nightmare that I would soon wake up from. Nothing was real, but it was also more real than anything I'd ever experienced. When we are in a life altering moment, I think that is kind of what happens. Time slows down and we see everything very clearly, as if we are watching it happen to someone else.

As I entered the room, I saw Jaron in the hospital bed with tubes in his nose and down his throat. He had black charcoal residue all over his face, chin, and chest, which is what the paramedics make you swallow for an overdose. The nurse was forcing a liquid through the tubes and flushing all the contents of his stomach out. This process, called gastric lavage, or stomach pumping, is not pleasant. I think the doctors and nurses make an effort to make it kind of brutal, because they don't want you back in their ER again the next week. The only way I can describe the smell in that room is that it smelled like death. I sat with my father for ten days while his life came to an end, and I was familiar with what death smelled like. It's a kind of sick, sour smell that is unmistakable and unforgettable.

I was able to keep it together and not cry, either because I was in shock, or because I was receiving help from above, or maybe a combination of both. The first thing I said to Jaron was, "Thank you for calling 911. I love you." He was crying, and telling me how sorry he was. He was still pretty out of it, and kept trying to explain what had happened. I told him it didn't matter, as long as he was all right. I was just so thankful that he was all right.

This day would later come to be known as the worst and the best day of my life. It was the worst day of my life, because I came very, very close to losing my son. It was horrifying, scary, miserable, and awful. But, it was also the best day of my life, because I didn't lose my son. He survived, and I was filled with immense gratitude for the miracle we had been granted that day.

Jaron had to stay in the hospital overnight for observation, and I stayed in the room with him. A medical assistant or orderly of some kind was assigned to stay in the room with us, as is protocol when a person has attempted suicide. I felt bad for the guy, having to just sit in a chair all night long while we held each other and talked and made half-hearted attempts to sleep.

Jaron was still not out of the woods. With an overdose, there can be all kinds of complications. There was a team of heart specialists monitoring his heart for damage from all of the meds. There was a team of internists watching all of his other organs for possible complications or failure. There was a team of respiratory therapists monitoring his oxygen saturation levels and breathing. There was a psychiatric team assigned to Jaron's case to assess whether or not he needed further evaluation, or if he needed to be put on a "72-hour psych hold."

The next morning we met with all the teams of doctors who determined that Jaron could be released to our care on the condition that he have an appointment with a psychiatrist before being discharged. We were able to bring him home that day and start him on the road to recovery.

Jaron had a long road of healing ahead of him, and we began by teaching his body how to swallow and absorb foods again. When he was brought into the emergency room, an intubation tube was forced down Jaron's throat to keep him alive and breathing. In ideal circumstances, this is performed under anesthesia because it is very painful. However, in the emergency situation he was in, the tube had to be inserted while Jaron was wide-awake. Being a singer, Jaron was worried about what this would do to his vocal chords, but thankfully, there was no lasting damage. It did take some time, however, for his body to readjust to eating and drinking solid foods. As brutal as a suicide attempt can be, the efforts to save the person can be equally brutal, and can have traumatic and lingering effects on the body.

Gratitude was how I made it though that day and the weeks that followed, and it would continue to be a healing tool for my entire family, including Jaron. He later told me that in the weeks leading up to his suicide attempt, he had not been eating well. He had been neglecting his body, pushing it to its absolute limits, depriving it of nutrition, sleep, rest, and exercise. For two days prior to his suicide attempt, he had hardly eaten at all. He believed his body had allowed his mind to do this violent thing because of the extremely weakened state it was in.

Learning to feel gratitude for his body, for the gift of life, and for those who were there to help him that day was a huge step in helping Jaron heal from this horrible event. I truly believe that gratitude and finding a way to feel thankful, and to express that thankfulness, was what got us through that experience. Our family was forever changed that day, but looking back, we can see we were changed for the better. We grew closer to one another, we learned to appreciate the fragility of life, and we became more grateful for each day we have on this earth together.

I often wonder if I would have been able to make it through that horrible day if I had not been actively practicing gratitude in my daily life. I believe that I was given the strength I needed at the very moment I needed it because gratitude had become such a significant part of my life, and it was a way for me to see through the darkness and know that the light was still there. From this experience, I learned that gratitude is much more than an attitude. It is a power. When you feel grateful, when you truly feel it in the depth of your soul, you are moved to action. You express gratitude to everything and everyone that helps or lifts you in any way. It is this power that transforms us into more than we thought we could be, and makes life infinitely sweeter.

*"Gratitude's magical power increases the natural flow
of health to the mind and body, and can assist the
body in healing more quickly, as countless studies have
shown. The magical power of gratitude also works
hand in hand with good bodily care, nutrition, and any
medical assistance you might have chosen to follow.*

*When there is some kind of sickness or condition in your body,
it is understandable that you may have negative feelings
about it, like worry, frustration, or fear. But having negative
feelings about sickness does not restore health. In fact, it has
the opposite effect—it reduces health even more. To increase
your health, you need to replace the negative feelings with
good feelings, and gratitude is the easiest way to do it."*
(Rhonda Byrne, "The Magic", p. 150)

Love and Accept Who You Are

Learning to love, accept, and appreciate my body led me to
another discovery—I needed to love *everything* about who
I was. Besides hating so many things about my physical
appearance, I had also spent a lot of time criticizing parts
of my personality that I didn't think were up to snuff. I
chose to believe and dwell on the negative things people
would say from time to time, and ignore most of the
compliments I would receive. I had a "No, I'm not" for every
nice thing someone said about me. At first glance, it may
have seemed I was just being humble, but really, I wasn't

giving myself enough credit for anything I did or said. The more I remained focused on the negative, and what I thought were unacceptable aspects of my personality, the worse I felt about myself. In fact, it was making me miserable, and, I believe, contributing to my overall feeling of un-wellness.

As part of my gratitude practice, I started trying to think of aspects of my personality, character, and nature that I was thankful for. This turned out to be as hard, if not harder, than feeling gratitude for my physical self. It is extremely difficult for most of us to sit down and really think about ourselves for very long in a positive way. Most of the time, our minds are filled with thoughts of what we should be doing, or what we did or said wrong, or what we didn't do or say that we should have. We just don't spend much time naturally focusing on what is good about us, what we did right, or how we may have influenced another person in a positive way. Nevertheless, I knew this was something I needed to do, so I decided to give it a shot.

I started out by making a list of good qualities I felt that I possessed. Again—super hard. I consoled myself by thinking no one would ever have to see the list, so no one could ever think I was conceited or "stuck on myself." I could always burn the list or toss it in the garbage once I was done. Why was making a list of my good qualities so hard? One reason may be that from the time I was a little girl, I can remember adults I looked up to speaking to each other about how So-and-So was such a conceited person, or about how What's-his-Name thought much too highly of himself. And I got the message: liking yourself too much is bad. Better not be too confident, too "stuck up", or too cocky. I think this is a message many of us probably received as children, which may have been helpful or useful at the time, but at this point in my life, it was no longer helpful, useful, or needed. In fact, it was holding me back in a big way.

The first good quality I came up with about myself was "organized." "Wow!" I thought, "Don't go too crazy now! People might think you have a big head!" The next quality was "compassionate. "Still pretty safe and generic. No one could call me conceited for being compassionate. As the list went on, and knowing that no one was ever going to see it anyway, I was able to dig a little deeper. I wrote down words like loving, generous, funny, intelligent, kind, and articulate. These were qualities that deep down I knew I possessed, but I had never allowed myself to focus on them for very long. It was scary to admit it, but I was a pretty great person, and had a lot to offer to the world.

But what about all those negative personality traits; the quirks, the oddities, the annoying things about me? After giving it some thought, I realized that I had to bring gratitude to those as well. If I was going to do this, if I was going to really love and accept myself fully, I had to love every part of me, warts and all. Just as I couldn't hold back on listing my wonderful and endearing qualities, I couldn't go easy on myself with the not-so-wonderful and unpleasant ones either. As Dr. Martin Luther King Jr. said, *"Darkness cannot drive out darkness: only light can do that."* I had to shine a light on the darkest parts of myself, and in the process allow them to heal.

It was somewhat easier to come up with the content for this list because I think it is in our nature as humans to dwell on our faults and weaknesses. What was harder, however, was to feel grateful for those parts of myself that I didn't like, to be thankful for how the ugly parts of me had taught me lessons I needed to learn and helped me to change for the better. Keeping that in mind, I tried to be brutally honest, but not brutal. In other words, I made an effort to not become so carried away in listing the negative qualities that I lost sight of all the positive traits I had just acknowledged. This was not about having a pity party or a self-hate session. I just wanted to honestly accept who I was, the good and the not so good.

In the book, "The Shadow Effect", Debbie Ford describes why we must honestly evaluate and embrace our flaws and weaknesses. She says, *"...whatever we have hidden away in shame or denied out of fear holds the key to unlock a self that we feel proud of, a self that inspires us, a self that is propelled into action by great vision and purpose rather than the one that is created out of our limitations and the unhealed wounds of our past.*

According to Ford, we can learn a lot about ourselves by examining those very traits, habits, and attributes that we dislike—those aspects of our personality we try to conceal, and hope and pray nobody ever finds out about. By exploring our not so pleasant side, we learn how to be a little more understanding and tolerant. She says that our darkness *"exists to point out where we are still incomplete, to teach us love, compassion and forgiveness--not just for others, but also for ourselves."*

So I began making my list. I started with what I felt were the easy ones, like, "Sometimes I am selfish," and "I care too much about my appearance." Then I listed personality traits that I found unacceptable, like, "I laugh at inappropriate times," "I think I always have to be in control," and "I never know what to say to people." Next, I listed all the stupid mistakes I could remember making throughout my life, the ones that lingered in my memory and haunted me still to this day. Next to each memory I wrote how that mistake or situation had made me feel and still made me feel when I thought about it—afraid, angry, ashamed, guilty, or resentful. I knew that increasing my faith could heal whatever I felt fearful about, because faith is the opposite of fear. Asking for forgiveness from the person I had hurt and/or from God could heal whatever I felt ashamed of or guilty about. And whatever I felt angry or resentful about could be healed by my willingness to forgive others.

Through this process, I realized one of the biggest things that annoyed me about myself was my lack of confidence. This is what I wrote in my journal at that time: "A weakness I have always felt trapped by is a lack of self-confidence. I do not believe that I will ever be good enough in the eyes of the world. I have tried to gain more confidence by looking perfect on the outside (which is impossible), having a perfectly clean and organized home (also impossible), having a perfect family (not), getting a job that proves I have worth (didn't work), by buying things (only brings temporary satisfaction), and reading self-help books (helped somewhat). Each of these attempts to gain self-confidence made me feel even worse about myself because I could not make myself feel confident and secure with whom I am. What looks on the outside to be pride is really an inward struggle to feel good about myself, to recognize my own worth, and to love and accept myself."

It occurred to me that for years I had been running around trying to look and act and be "perfect" on the outside, while on the inside I was a ball of anxiety, fear, stress and doubts. I was like that country song that says, "Put on your lipstick girl, and hide the crazy!" I thought that if I looked good enough on the outside, no one would know how messed up, scared, and sad I was on the inside. And I guess for the most part, it had worked. Except there was one person I wasn't fooling—me. By running away from the things I didn't like about myself, I was creating my own fake little world where nothing was as it seemed and all my energy went into keeping up the facade. By refusing to accept and love myself exactly as I was, I wasn't living an authentic life. Now here I was, making my list and acknowledging to myself that I was NOT perfect, that I DID have flaws and weaknesses, that I HAD made mistakes in my life, and that it was okay. I was still a good person. I could forgive myself, love myself, and accept myself right here and now, imperfections and all.

I remembered that a friend of mine, who was also my chiropractor and, basically, our family doctor, had taught me a mantra. He had me to repeat to myself several times daily, "I totally and completely love and accept myself as I am right now." This healing statement helped me remember to cut myself some slack, and allowed me to finally start feeling genuine gratitude for all the parts of myself I had tried to conceal or deny for so long.

> *"Talking to my therapist one day, I was sharing*
> *with him that I felt in a very negative place. I*
> *told him I was in a place of self-loathing.*
> *He asked me, "What is your case against yourself?"*
> *I said, "I hate myself because I'm so negative." I could*
> *see the irony, but I couldn't laugh. Or maybe I did.*
> *He suggested that I try something. "Be in the flow*
> *of gratitude," he said. "Whenever you are having*
> *that kind of negative thought, go into naming*
> *all the things you have to be grateful for."*

And I found that technique to be very powerful. For hours, I'd been on a rampage of negativity, but as soon as I began the flow of gratitude, it was as though my shadow disappeared the way the wicked witch melted when Dorothy threw water on her. And it was the same phenomenon really. The shadow isn't even real. It just appears so. And as soon as it's exposed to the light, then the darkness disappears. The problem then, was not just the presence of my negativity, but the absence of my positivity! As soon as I filled my mind with gratitude, the shadow trait of self-hatred could no longer exist. In the presence of love, fear is gone."
(Marianne Williamson, "The Shadow Effect" p. 156)

Neale Donald Walsh said, *"The struggle ends when gratitude begins."* I could finally feel my own personal struggle coming to an ending because of the gratitude practices I had incorporated into my daily life. The healing had started—I I was overcoming the self-doubts, fears, anxieties, and destructive behaviors that had been controlling me. I know it doesn't really make sense, but I was grateful for gratitude. It transformed me in more ways than I could count. My body felt younger, healthier, and more energized than it had in years; my mind was clearer; I was happier and had a more positive outlook on life; my days were filled with good experiences and positive relationships instead of worry and stress; life was not such a struggle anymore. Practicing gratitude brought more peace, contentment, and love into my life, and I could not wait to share that love with others.

Express Love and Gratitude to Others ▩▩▩▩▩

For a big portion of my life, I had a hard time telling people that I loved them. I don't really know why, but it just seemed like a hard thing to say. It was kind of a scary thing to express my feelings so openly. In my family, we rarely, if ever, said the words, "I love you." I knew for sure that I was loved, but that knowledge came from the loving *actions* of my parents and grandparents. I guess they felt as though they didn't need to say it, because they showed it. I think they were partly right, because I never doubted that I was loved and cherished. But once in a while, I longed to hear them say it to me. So years later, when I had a family of my own, my husband and I made an effort to express our love for each other vocally, and we also would tell our boys that we loved them, but it was not a regular occurrence. "I love you" seemed to be a phrase that was reserved mostly for special occasions or times of sadness.

Then one day, when my kids were still quite young, I went to the funeral of a young woman who had been killed in a car accident. She and her sister had been driving home from a concert late at night. Her sister, who was driving, had gotten distracted and had run off the road. The young woman was thrown from the car and killed instantly. Her sister survived the crash. Witnessing the devastation and raw anguish of this family was heartbreaking, and I left that funeral determined to tell my children every single day that I loved them. And I did. Whether I felt like saying it or not, whether they were in the mood to hear it or not, I started saying, "I love you," whenever my children were walking out the door. We started including family hugs and saying "I love you," to each other at night after prayers, and saying it before hanging up the phone with each other. Pretty soon, my kids got used to it. I think at first they thought I was a little crazy, but it became a normal thing. I even started saying "I love you" to my parents at the end of phone conversations and upon leaving their home for a visit. Before long, they were saying it back to me! My parents were vocalizing their love for me, something I never thought they would do. Now it is unusual if any of my children hang up the phone or leave the house without saying, "Love you, Mom!" and I couldn't be more thrilled.

It shouldn't be hard to tell the people you love that you love them. However, if it is difficult for you, or if it's something you have just never done, the best way to get over the fear is to do it. And the best person to start with is yourself. Try looking at yourself in the mirror and speaking aloud the words, "I love you". After you have stopped laughing, try saying it again. Then say it over and over again until you actually believe it. Yes, this is a very strange thing to do, and you will probably feel a little silly when you do it, but here is why this is important: words are extremely powerful. When you vocally declare something, you are literally speaking it into existence. This is why we should be extremely careful with our words and how we use them.

Words can be a powerful weapon we can use to tear down, afflict, and demean others and ourselves, or they can be used to promote sacred, meaningful, tender exchanges with the people in our lives. Saying the words, "I love you," is one of the simplest yet most profound things you can do for someone. It might be a scary thing to do at first, but the more you do it the easier it becomes. You will never regret the expressions of love you give to others.

Saying, "Thank You," is another powerful way to express our love and appreciation to others. A few weeks after the Worst and Best Day, I had the impression that I needed to show my gratitude to those medical professionals who had worked so hard to save my son's life. In particular, I owed a debt of gratitude to the paramedics who arrived so quickly after Jaron called 911. Their fast response time was crucial to my son's survival. They also administered the charcoal to him immediately to begin absorbing the many pills and medications he had ingested. Without this treatment, Jaron's heart, brain, or other organs could have been severely damaged, or shut down completely.

I was extremely thankful to the nurse who had stayed with Jaron in the ER as well, pumping fluids into his body and being tough but gentle with him. She didn't show sympathy, but she was compassionate and attentive. The other person I needed to thank was the young medical resident who helped me get an appointment with a psychiatrist for Jaron.

He even went as far as to give me his personal cell phone number and told me to call him whenever I needed to.

I made a couple of gift baskets and printed out a picture of our family that had been taken just days after that ordeal. I wrote a note of gratitude to the strangers who had given me back my son just by doing their jobs. Then I asked my husband to drive me to the hospital.

Walking back into that emergency room, I felt a flood of emotions, but this was not about me. I knew I had to thank these wonderful people. I could not rest until I let them know how extremely grateful I was to them. The nurse who helped Jaron was on duty that day, and the receptionist called her to the lobby to speak with us. As I hugged her and thanked her for helping to save my son, she expressed gratitude to me for coming. She had not been having a good day; in fact, it had been a pretty rotten one. She told us it was one of those days that she had been considering walking out and never coming back. We had shown up just at the right time with our simple gift basket and homemade thank you card, and helped her see the importance of the work she was doing. Hearing those words made my heart fill up with even more gratitude. We asked her to share her gift basket with the paramedics who had been on call that day, and said goodbye.

Next, we set off to find the medical resident that helped us and had been so compassionate towards our son. I hate to say it, but most doctors just don't seem to have much desire to get personally involved in their patient's lives. I suppose if they did, they would be overwhelmed with trying to help everyone. But I guess this one young doctor had been moved by our situation, and had gone beyond his job description to help us out. After searching all over the hospital for him, we finally just left the gift basket and note in his office. I don't know how he felt about receiving our simple gift, but I know how wonderful I felt after expressing my gratitude, and how awful I would have felt if I hadn't.

Someone once said, *"Life is short. There is no time to leave important words unsaid."* I believe this statement to be true. I also believe there are many things that we could leave unsaid and be the better for it. Sarcastic remarks, stupid jokes, careless comments, and insinuations can tear people down faster than almost anything else. After I had been practicing daily gratitude for a while, I became more aware that from time to time I would make off-hand comments to myself or sometimes to my husband that were not exactly uplifting or supportive of others. In fact, at times they were downright mean spirited and uncalled for. I can't even count how many times I have made a derogatory comment about a television personality's hair or outfit, and rationalized that it wasn't so bad because I didn't actually know them and they would never hear what I was saying anyway. Or, how often I felt justified in tearing down someone who had said something hurtful to or about me, or whom I perceived had injured me, mostly my pride, in some way. If I wanted to take my gratitude practice to the next level and use it to spread love to others, I had to completely stop speaking ill of others, even those I didn't know personally, or those I felt deserved it. I had to stop making sarcastic remarks and jokes, and use words that were more uplifting, helpful, and positive.

I remember one instance when I went to a choir practice for my church choir. I came in a little late and quickly took a seat at the end of the row. The choir director asked me if I could move down and take the seat next to a neighbor of mine who I felt I knew fairly well. I guess I must have been in a silly mood or something, because I said, "No, I can't do that." When the director asked me why, I replied, "Well, I don't really like her." The whole room gasped. I guess it sounded a lot funnier in my head. I quickly apologized and said I was totally kidding, but I felt terrible. I found out later that this lady was feeling like no one in the neighborhood liked her and that she had recently been treated badly by a few of the women in our area. My off-handed remark had deepened a wound that was already hurting, and I learned how damaging words could be, even when we think we are being funny.

As I continued to look for more ways to show love and appreciation for others, I decided to look around at the people I most admired—the friends and family members I considered the most kind and loving. What traits or qualities did they possess that I could try to emulate? After giving this some thought, I realized that the people I most enjoyed being around had one thing in common—they listened to me. When I spoke to them, they looked me in the eye, and they really listened. They weren't checking their cell phone for messages. They weren't just waiting for me to stop talking so they could say what they wanted to say. They weren't trying to "one-up" me with a better story than the one I just told. They just really listened. They also asked follow-up questions. In other words, these people were not just sitting passively while I did all the talking. They showed genuine interest in what I was saying by asking questions, staying engaged in the conversation, and even, at times, repeating what I said to make sure they understood correctly. Being around this type of person made me feel validated, important, and respected. I wanted to try to do better at listening to others when they spoke to me, and in that way show them I really cared.

I knew I appreciated those people who listened to me when I talked, but how often was I supporting others by being a good listener for them? I realized it was probably not often enough, and I needed to work on my listening skills. The existentialist philosopher and theologian Paul Tillich said, *"The first duty of love is to listen."* If we sincerely want to demonstrate love to others, we need to listen to them. So how do we learn to become better listeners? Most of us may think we are really good listeners, but I believe we are all guilty at times of being that distracted, interrupting, or one-upping friend. I sat down and made a list of some of the dos and don'ts of being a good listener.

Good listeners:

- Make eye contact
- Ask questions/clarify
- Hear the message behind the words
- Stay present
- Don't try to solve your problems
- Don't make it about themselves
- Don't interrupt
- Don't assume they know what you're going to say

It was not always easy trying to remember to stay focused, make eye contact, look for the meaning behind the words, and ask relevant questions. But the hardest thing of all for me was not interrupting. I found that when I had a thought I wanted to share in a conversation, I wanted to share it right away before I forgot it. I also had a long held belief that I was the type of person who tends to get ignored, and if I wanted to be heard I had to boldly assert myself in conversations. I soon learned, however, that if I resisted the urge to interrupt and respectfully let the person talking finish their thought, they were more likely to listen to what I had to say when it was my turn. And even if I never got to share that great story or idea I thought was so important, it was okay.

Happily, I found trying to be a better listener helped me to become a better conversationalist, which was one of the undesirable traits I had listed about myself; "I never know what to say to people." Because I was not focusing on me, but was instead giving my complete attention to the other person, I became less stressed out about having conversations with people. And since having someone listen to them made people feel validated, they were more than happy to talk to me!

Bringing more gratitude into my life has taught me to love and appreciate the magnificent gift of my body and all that it does for me each and every day. I experienced much more healing in my body by giving it love, compassion, and acceptance than I had ever been able to achieve by hating it. Feeling gratitude for all aspects of my personality, the good and the not-so-good, taught me that there is absolutely no excuse for belittling myself or anyone else. It feels much better to express words of love and appreciation than to say hurtful, negative things. Keeping sarcastic comments or stupid jokes to myself is much more empowering than saying something I would most likely regret later. And being a gracious listener is way better than being the person who never seems to run out of things to say.

Viewing others with the eyes of love and gratitude allows us to see them, and ourselves, as we really are. Each one of us is an important child of God and each of us deserves to be treated with respect. When we remember that, we feel lighter, happier, and better about ourselves and about life. We don't have time to criticize ourselves or anyone else because we are too busy enjoying the most amazing, beautiful, magnificent life imaginable.

CREATE THE HABITS

Be Grateful for Your Body:

1. Record in a journal every day ten things you are grateful for and why. Include one thing about your body that you are grateful for. Gradually work up to making a list of ten amazing things about your body that you are thankful for.

2. As soon as your eyes open in the morning, use that as a signal to begin feeling gratitude. Make a mental list of the things you have to be grateful for before you get out of bed. If you fall back asleep, start the list over again.

3. Write a letter of gratitude to your body. List all of the aspects of it you are grateful for and express how you will nurture and care for it from now on.

Love and Accept Who You Are:

1. Make a list of all your positive attributes. Don't hold back. Allow yourself to truly appreciate the wonderful aspects of your personality. Remember

that God has blessed you with the amazing gift of your body and mind, and feel deep gratitude for those blessings.

2. Make a list of all the things you don't like about yourself. Feel compassion for yourself and realize you do not have to be a perfect person. Feel gratitude for how the unpleasant parts of yourself have helped you be a better, more compassionate and understanding person.

3. Make a list of all the mistakes you have made in your life that you still carry with you. Next to each one, write down the emotion that memory invokes: fear, shame, guilt, resentment, anger, etc. Allow yourself to now be thankful for the lessons you learned from those mistakes, and give those emotions permission to leave you.

Express Love and Gratitude to Others:

1. Say, "I love you," often. Practice saying it to yourself in the mirror until you believe it. Verbally express love to your family and friends in conversations, when hanging up the phone, or when leaving them. Write a love note to your partner or spouse and hide it somewhere they will find it at a later time.

2. Say, "thank you," and express sincere appreciation to those who serve, lift, and support you. Make a small gift basket, a batch of cookies, or a hand

written note and take it to someone who has been helpful or kind to you recently.

3. Refrain from sarcastic remarks, hurtful jokes, snide comments, and any negative self-talk. When you catch yourself wanting to say something negative or unkind, use that as a cue to be more compassionate and understanding.

4. Be a good listener. When someone speaks to you, put down your cell phone, look them in the eye, zip up your lips, and really listen.

Affirmations:

- My body is an amazing gift from God and I treat it with love and respect.
- My gratitude for my body leads me to make healthy choices that nourish my body and spirit.
- I love and respect others and myself enough to keep cruel comments to myself.
- I am a good listener. People love to talk to me because I really hear what they have to say.
- I easily express love and appreciation to others.
- I realize that I have made mistakes in my life, and that they have taught me to be more kind, compassionate, and tolerant of others.

Use this space to write your own gratitude habits and affirmations:

Habit # 2: Learning

"The heart of the prudent getteth knowledge; and the ear of the wise seeketh knowledge." Proverbs 18:15

Learn What Truly Feeds You

When I was a little girl, I loved playing with Barbies. My best friend and I would spend hours and hours in our make-believe Barbie world—dressing them, combing their hair, and making up stories about them. What were their husbands like? How many kids did they have? Where did they live? What jobs did they have? What type of cars did they drive? We would even try to stay up all night on the weekends just so we could play that much longer. We didn't want to do anything else. Playing with our dolls was more important than sleeping, eating, riding our bikes, running around outside, or participating in any other game. We were creating something we were passionate about, and we were enthralled with it.

My friend and I didn't know it at the time, but we had found an activity that truly "fed" us—a pursuit we loved doing so much everything else became secondary. The joy we experienced as a result of our creativity was almost addictive—it was so enjoyable we never wanted to stop. I think when we become adults, most of us forget about these kinds of activities. We grow up. We become serious. Reality takes over and there is work to be done. There is little, if any, time for the activities that allow our imaginations to soar and our minds to relax into pure joy. We forget to nourish that inventive part of ourselves we tapped into so freely as children. But if all we ever do is the work that needs to be done, life becomes routine, boring, and mundane.

Although it is true accomplishing our work and checking items off our "to do" list does bring a sense of satisfaction, for the most part, doing our daily tasks does not take much mental stretching. We already know how to do those things, so we do them almost mindlessly, as if we are on autopilot. There is also a kind of "safeness" in sticking to the tasks that don't really challenge us or require much thought on our part. For example, I remember when I decided to go back to work after years of being a stay at home mom, I found a job as a dental assistant with a doctor who was willing to train me. There was so much to learn and remember in my new work environment I felt overwhelmed at times, but one part of my job came very easily to me—doing the laundry. At the end of each day, all the employees would change into their street clothes and leave their uniforms at the office. The next day there would be a few loads of laundry waiting for me. Well, this was one area where I felt totally qualified—I had become an expert at doing laundry as a mother. But sometimes I became so focused on doing the laundry, I would forget to clean the instruments or prepare the room for the next patient. I was doing the thing that was the easiest for me, the thing that felt safe, rather than focusing on learning new skills.

A fact of life is that there will always be things that demand our attention. Task after task will present itself, and, if we are not diligent, we will end up neglecting the parts of ourselves that long to create, learn, imagine, and dream. Most of the time, there is no real challenge to the mundane and routine tasks of life, and, therefore, no real growth. I believe it is crucial to our emotional, spiritual, and physical health to take time now and then to become totally engrossed in a project that inspires, excites, and thrills us. How much better would we feel if instead of turning to the food we eat to fill our emotional needs, we created a beautiful work of art, wrote our life story, planned an amazing party, or started a collection? Doing something that exhilarates and even scares us a little may be just the medicine we need.

In a letter to his eleven year old son, Albert Einstein once wrote, *"That is the way to learn the most...when you are doing something with such enjoyment that you don't notice that the time passes."* In the 1970s, this phenomenon was termed being in "the flow" by psychologist Mihaly Csikszentmihalyi. He found that people who were totally engaged in a pursuit had changes in their brain chemistry and breathing patterns that actually improved their physical health and sense of well-being. He also found that in order for an activity to *keep* us in the flow, it must be challenging but not overwhelming. In other words, it must keep us interested and engaged, but at the same time be slightly difficult to master. I knew that I needed more opportunities to get into "the flow," to do things I truly enjoyed, and to try my hand at a few new things that would challenge me as well.

> *"I am always doing that which I cannot do, in*
> *order that I may learn how to do it."*
> *– Pablo Picasso*

Do More of What You Love

As part of my quest to create more healing habits in my life, I wanted to do things I loved doing more often. I longed for more soul feeding activities in my daily life. As an adult, I had become a worker, and I would only "play" if there were time left over after all the work was done. There usually was not. And even if there was, I was usually too tired anyway. I felt not taking the time to do things I truly loved—that fed me emotionally and spiritually—was sucking the joy from my life and making me into an extremely boring person. Besides that, I also learned "all work and no play" was bad for my health. People who report being bored with life have been shown to be at a greater risk for developing eating disorders, alcoholism, depression, anxiety, hostility, anger, and drug addiction. I was anxious to start learning to be more playful and relaxed. I wanted to feel the excitement of being creative again.

I set a goal to make time for creativity, play and fun; but what did I really enjoy doing? It had been a long time since I had actually given any thought to what brought me joy, so it was hard to think of things at first. I decided I should start by looking at the ways I spent my free time. What did I do when I didn't *have* to do anything? What were those activities I could do for hours and hours on end without getting sick of them? What were my "soul feeders"? I sat down to make my list. Just now while writing this, I realized making lists must be one of the things I enjoy because I do it so often.

MY "SOUL FEEDERS":

- Organizing stuff
- Decorating my house
- Learning new things
- Studying spiritual topics and taking notes

- Writing in my gratitude journal with colored pens
- Sitting quietly and drinking tea
- Reading self-help books
- Watching my favorite TV shows
- Singing in the car
- Watching my sons perform
- Hanging out at the bookstore
- Doing family history research
- Going camping/boating with my family
- Playing with make-up
- Shopping with my mom and sister

Upon completing my list and looking back over it, my first thought was, "Okay, I'm kind of a boring person! What kind of person likes to organize things? How lame is that?" Then I remembered my commitment to love all aspects of myself, and that included the parts I deemed a little dull, so I pressed the stop button on the self-criticism track that was playing in my mind. True, many of the things on my list were not the most exciting activities in the world, but they were the things I truly enjoyed. I could have made a list of things that others might find far more adventurous and thrilling, but it would not have been an accurate reflection of what I actually found appealing. I wondered why these activities were so important to me; what was it about doing them that was so enjoyable? After some thought, I came to the conclusion these things I loved doing, the things that fed my soul, did so because I felt the most like myself when I was doing them. I was more myself when I was with my mom and my sister shopping or when I was with my family at the lake than I was at any other time. I didn't have to try to be anything different than what I was, or make an impression or struggle to fit in. I was in a relaxed, easy state of mind, and it felt wonderful.

I wanted to incorporate more of my most loved activities into my daily life. I wanted to take time every day to do those things that brought me true joy and fulfillment. There were some things on the list that I could not do every day, like going boating with my family or shopping with my mom and sister. Those were activities I could plan in advance to do every month or so, and part of the enjoyment would be having them to look forward to. Some activities could be done on a weekly basis, such as doing family history research or hanging out at the bookstore. There were a few, like watching my sons perform and decorating my home, which would have to wait until the occasion presented itself. But all the other items on my list could pretty much be practiced daily. I felt my life would be richer, more meaningful, and more enjoyable if I did several things from my list each day.

One of the activities on my list I particularly enjoyed was studying spiritual topics and writing about what I had learned in my study journal. I also really loved recording my thoughts in my gratitude journal using colored markers and pens. In order to incorporate more of my soul feeders into my life, I decided to combine these two and do them together on a daily basis. I found my attitude and outlook on life was much better if I woke up at 5:30 a.m., (an hour before I wake my son up for school) and spent that time studying, pondering, journaling, meditating, praying, and practicing gratitude. This has become what I call my Morning Sacred Time. It is my one-hour a day when I can fill up my heart with uplifting words, positive affirmations, grateful thoughts, and loving feelings. It feeds my soul in ways that nothing else can. I also know I won't be interrupted by phone calls, visitors, or other distractions at this time of day, so I can give my full attention to what I am studying or contemplating.

My Morning Sacred Time is something I not only look forward to every day, but I actually feel sort of lost and out of whack if I skip it. This is my time to ground myself, get reconnected to my source of strength, and to refuel my spirit and mind. Once I got into the habit of taking this hour each morning, it became non-negotiable. No matter what else needs to be done each day, my Morning Sacred Time is the one thing that I will absolutely not skip.

I was able to work most of the other soul feeders into my daily routine by simply paying a little more attention to how I spent my time. One of my favorite things to do is to organize—whether it be the refrigerator, the office, the junk drawer, or the clothes in my closet, organizing just helps everything make a little bit more sense to me. I guess it's just how my brain works, or maybe it's because I'm a control freak, but either way, organizing makes me happy. Life is always presenting me with opportunities to create order out of chaos, especially in my role as a mother, so I didn't really need to make extra time for organizing. What I did try to do was enjoy the process of organizing as much as I enjoyed the end result. I felt taking joy in the journey was an important aspect of learning and feeding my soul.

I also set aside an extra ten minutes each morning to sit quietly and drink a cup of herbal tea after my Morning Sacred Time and before turning on the TV to watch the news. It felt luxurious to take that time in the morning to just sit, reflect, and sip my tea while looking out my window at the trees, or, on a warm day, sitting outside on my deck. It was a way for my soul to connect with nature and to enjoy the stillness that can only be found in the early morning hours.

Some other ways I incorporated my soul feeders into my daily routine:

1. I kept several self-help books on my nightstand so I could read a few pages before going to sleep at night, and I always took one with me if I knew I was going somewhere I would have to wait, like a dentist appointment or a visit to the doctor's office.
2. I recorded our favorite television programs and watched them at night with my husband as a way to unwind after a busy or hectic day.

3. I put all my favorite songs on my iPod so I could sing my head off in the car whenever I was driving somewhere.

4. Since I love playing with make-up, I allowed myself enough time in the morning to carefully apply my foundation, eye shadows, and mascara without worrying about how long it took. This was a part of my day I enjoyed, so I did not want to rush through it.

It felt good to give myself permission to do the things that fed my soul and renewed my spirit, and I wanted to know how other people did it too. I asked some of my close friends and family members what their soul feeders were. What activities did they spend their time doing that helped them feel alive, creative, or just authentically themselves? Here are a few of the responses I received:

- Fishing
- Golfing
- Talking with people
- Going to yoga class
- Making a home-cooked meal
- Snowboarding
- Refinishing furniture
- Being outside in nature
- Walking the dog
- Reading a good book
- Dancing around the house

- Doodling
- Making people smile
- Hanging out with good friends
- Going for a drive

I also love this response that I got from a dear friend of mine:

"A few things that truly make me happy and keep me grounded are writing letters or sending a card, and expressing love and gratitude to others. Nothing makes me happier than when I am serving others even in the smallest ways. And exercise is my best outlet to a clear mind and a better me. Good food never hurt my soul either!" -- Aimee K.

Every one of us has our own way of accessing our source of pure joy and contentment. By making our soul feeders a priority, we give ourselves permission to be uniquely ourselves. There is no need to feel guilty about taking the time to do the things that we love, because those are the best and healthiest things we can ever do. When we are feeding our souls with what makes us feel most alive and passionate, we are connecting with our deepest, most authentic selves. And, just as Albert Einstein once told his son, we really do learn the most when we are totally immersed in doing something we love.

"When the student is ready, the teacher will appear."
-- Buddha

Try New Things

Learning new things was on the top of my soul feeder list, but what was I actually doing in order to learn and grow? Was I really making an effort to develop new skills, or was I sticking to those activities I already knew how to do fairly well? Was I striving to expand my mind and challenge myself, or was I playing it safe and sticking to the routine? There is a card game called Low Ball, in which the players try to win the game by collecting the lowest cards possible. The person with the least points at the end of the game wins. In a way, I felt like I was playing low ball in my life, never taking a chance on going for all the points. I wanted to make learning new things a higher priority in my life, and I knew that if I did, one or more of the following would happen:

1. My life would become more full and interesting
2. I would become a more interesting and joyful person
3. I would feel better mentally and physically

The philosopher Aristotle pointed out the difference between momentary pleasure (hedonia) and the pleasure that comes from learning new ideas and developing new skills (eudaimonia). He taught that true happiness comes from living a virtuous life, doing work that is worth doing, and realizing our human potential. Aristotle believed that learning was the key to happiness. If I could open my mind to new activities, ideas, and concepts, maybe I would feel happier and more satisfied with life in general. If I learned to try new things, even those I wasn't sure I would like, maybe I would create some fun and excitement that wasn't there before. I even had the inkling that learning and growing would not only improve my mental health, but my physical health as well. When I looked deeper into this, I found out that studies among the elderly have shown that learning new concepts and ideas decreased the risk of developing Alzheimer's disease and dementia. Recent research even suggests that the feeling of satisfaction that comes from learning something new can lower the body's levels of the stress hormone cortisol. It also contributes to better sleep and improved immune function.

As I said earlier, one of the first things I did on my path to wellness was to learn all I could about natural health and nutrition. In the past, the way I had approached food was not healthy or natural. I didn't think I enjoyed cooking, so most of the time I turned to pre-packaged foods that took little time to prepare and also contained little, if any, nutritional value. Now I knew better, and I needed to learn how to prepare foods that were nourishing, wholesome and nutritious. I knew if cooking this new way was too time consuming or complex I wouldn't stick with it, so I searched for ways to make simple, healthy versions of what I had already been making. For example, instead of frozen chicken nuggets, we could easily cook some chicken tenderloins on the grill. Instead of boxed mac & cheese, I could throw some short grain brown rice in the rice cooker and it would be done in almost the same amount of time. Instead of buying pre-chopped iceberg lettuce from a bag, with a little more effort I could prepare a delicious kale salad and lemon vinaigrette dressing. It did take more time to prepare our meals this way, but I found that if I planned our menu in advance and bought all the ingredients at the beginning of the week, I could spend less time staring into the pantry wondering what to prepare for dinner and more time in the actual preparation. It was simply a matter of thinking ahead and making the effort.

I also noticed that I had to go easy on myself as I learned a new way of cooking and eating. Sometimes my efforts to feed my family healthy, home-cooked meals led to frustrating experiences in the kitchen. There were times when my kids would say things like: "Good try Mom, but you don't need to make that again," or "That was good, it just wasn't my favorite," and "Could we just have Hamburger Helper next time?" My husband, bless his heart, never did say anything—he knows better! Trying to become a better, healthier cook was, and still is, a process of trial and error, but I have learned not to take myself too seriously, and to laugh when things don't turn out exactly right. Joseph B. Wirthlin once said, *"When you are tempted to groan, you might try to laugh instead. It will extend your life and make the lives of all those around you more enjoyable."* This is such an amazing piece of advice! If a dish comes out too dry, too sticky, too mushy, or just plain awful, it is okay. It is not the end of the world, nobody died, and I learned what not to do the next time. Another plus: I discovered that cooking is kind of fun! Once I gave myself permission to experiment, try new things, and even fail from time to time, it became a much more enjoyable experience.

Another concept I felt I needed to learn more about was listening to the wisdom of my body. I had spent many years despising my body, ignoring its signals, and taking it for granted. But now I had made the commitment to love, appreciate, and respect my body, and that included paying attention to what it was trying to tell me. In my training as a health coach, I learned that our bodies are constantly sending us messages about what they need, and it is up to us to interpret those messages and respond to them. In doing this, we create a partnership between our body and our spirit, opening the door to excellent health and vitality.

Once I learned this incredible truth, I felt a twinge of sadness for all those years my body had been sending me messages: fatigue, aches, pains, cravings, dryness, swelling, etc., and I had responded not in a loving, nurturing way, but with hatred and ingratitude. I had been so completely out of touch with my body for so long, I was not sure how I would begin to establish that connection. This brought to mind a friend of mine from years ago who was extremely tuned in to the messages and sensations of her body. We were both expecting our first child and would often compare notes about how we were feeling and what we were experiencing in our pregnancies. I remember her telling me that her baby was only kicking with one of its legs. "How could she possibly know that?" I thought to myself. I could feel my baby kicking, but I had no idea whether it was with one leg or the other. Sure enough, when her baby was born, he had a clubfoot, and had not moved that one leg throughout the entire nine-month period. I was amazed that my friend had been so in tune with her body that she was able to recognize something so subtle.

Now it was my turn to start listening to my body. I could no longer ignore, despise, or neglect it. I loved and respected my body now, and I wanted to give it what it needed in order to feel it's very best. But I also had to remember when I felt like eating another cookie or more chocolate, that was not my body's wisdom—that was a craving. I had to go a little deeper and figure out what was really going on in there. I started paying close attention to how my body felt after eating certain foods: did I feel bloated, tired, energized, sluggish, scattered? I explored my moods, emotions, and subtle aches and pains and tried to link them to what my body might be needing: rest, nutrition, movement, hydration, etc. Listening to my body turned out not to be as hard as I thought it would be. It was mostly a process of letting go of judgment and being honest with myself about what I was feeling.

One of the most obvious signals my body had been sending me for years was fatigue. I felt tired, worn down, and sluggish most of the time. In the past, I had responded to this message from my body by eating sugar, usually chocolate, and drinking caffeine laden carbonated sodas. I could see now that stuffing myself with sweets and stimulants was only giving me short bursts of energy, followed by even more fatigue and lethargy. Did my body have a caffeine and sugar deficiency? No. I needed to address the real problem and stop trying to mask it with artificial substances. In fact, the sugar and caffeine were making me feel worse, not better!

By turning to soda and sweets every time my energy was low, I was sending my blood sugar levels on a rollercoaster ride—soaring high for a short period of time, then plummeting back down so low it took consuming even more sugar to raise it up again. This can be a very dangerous cycle as low blood glucose levels, or hypoglycemia, can lead to loss of mental function, unconsciousness, and seizures. Blood glucose that is too high, or hyperglycemia, can also be associated with health risks and mental impairment. Because of the amount of sugar I was consuming, I experienced hypoglycemic symptoms like shakiness, sweating, and a racing heart on a regular basis. I knew I needed to get off the rollercoaster and get my blood sugar under control. For me, that meant giving up soda completely. I didn't feel like I could just drink it once in a while, because it really did feel like an addiction. If I didn't have a tall glass of Coke every morning by 10 a.m., I didn't feel "normal". Without it, I was grouchy, moody, and had a giant headache. No matter where I was or what I was doing, I had to have my morning soda. For any substance to be considered addictive, it has to meet two criteria: 1. There is a compulsive need to use it in order to function normally, and, 2. When it is unobtainable, the user suffers from withdrawal. I could see my soda consumption clearly fit into those parameters, and I needed to change. It was not easy, but I gave up drinking soda and switched to water. By doing that one simple thing, as well as finding healthier alternatives to candy and sweets, my blood sugar levels returned to normal, and I very rarely experienced those uncomfortable symptoms of hypoglycemia.

As I started paying more attention to the sensations of my body, I began to learn how it communicated to me. When I felt tired and run down, it often meant I had not had enough physical movement. I never really enjoyed exercising, sweating, or being out of breath, so most of my physical activity consisted of household chores and chasing my kids around. But once my kids were older, there was less chasing around to do, and I needed to find another way to keep moving. A friend of mine suggested I come to the yoga class she was teaching at the local recreation center twice a week, and since I couldn't think of a good excuse not to go, I went. By going to that class, I discovered a love for yoga I still have to this day. Long after attending that first class, I continue to practice yoga daily and it has become an important part of my daily routine. This same friend was also an aerobics instructor, and after I had been going to yoga for some time, she suggested I try coming to her step aerobics class. I was unsure and nervous about going to this class, but I told her I would try to come. I finally did go to the aerobics class, and guess what? I hated every minute of it! Every time my cute friend and instructor tried to help me by correcting me over her headset in front of the entire class, "Linda, you're facing the wrong way," or "Lift your knee higher, Linda," I felt humiliated, clumsy, and awkward. I could have toughed it out, kept trying to learn and maybe I would have come to enjoy it eventually, but I decided to listen to my inner wisdom and stick with a workout I really enjoyed, like yoga. When I look back on it now, I can laugh about how funny it was that I absolutely sucked at aerobics, and I feel really happy I tried something new, even if it turned out not to be for me.

Recently I decided to try golfing as a way to bring more physical activity and movement into my life. My husband, David, loves to golf, and had been inviting me to go with him for a long time. I resisted his invitations for years, because on the few occasions I did go, it was a frustrating and exhausting experience for me. It was frustrating because I could not hit the ball well, and exhausting because when I did manage to hit the ball, it didn't go very far, so I had to hit twice as many times as David did to get to the same place! But in my quest to learn new things, I felt I should give it another shot. David found an instructor who was patient and claimed to specialize in teaching non-athletic women, (um, that would be me), and so I began my lessons. After a few months of instruction from someone I was not married to (very important), I actually gained some skills and began to enjoy playing. I may not be a scratch golfer, but now I can at least hit the ball, and the best part is I get to spend time outside in the sun with the one I love. Being open to trying new activities I might not normally be drawn to has taught me I don't have to be perfect at something in order to enjoy it, and if I really don't enjoy it, I can always try something else.

Be on the Lookout for Your Teachers

I have often been guilty of thinking I can learn all I need to learn on my own. I have prided myself on being able to figure things out without help or assistance from anyone. If there is something I don't know how to do, I can read the manual or take a self-study course, or read a book or look it up on Google. But I have come to realize it isn't always possible or wise to go it alone. We must be willing to learn from sources other than ourselves if we truly want to grow. Each of us are given many teachers in our lives that are sent to show us something about ourselves or about our lives that needs to change. Sometimes those teachers are people. Sometimes they are situations. At times, they are painful experiences that force us to face a part of our inner selves we don't like very much. But each and every teacher that comes into our lives is a gift from God. He sends these teachers to us in order that we might grow, learn, develop, and eventually be transformed into who we are meant to be. Not unlike paying attention to the signals our bodies are sending us, we need to pay attention to and learn from the signals, or teachers, that show up in our lives.

I remember one day when my youngest son was about four years old. We were shopping at the mall, and Devin was tired, bored, and wanted to leave. Every time we passed an exit, he would exclaim, "There's a door! We could go out that way!" I still had shopping to do, and I was getting impatient with Devin and his anxiousness to go home. As I took him to the restrooms, I told him in a not-so-patient tone he needed a nap as soon as we got home. A woman who was in the restroom looked up at me and said sympathetically, "I think maybe Mommy needs a nap too." Her comment caught me off guard, and I realized at that moment I needed to change my attitude and the way I was speaking to my precious son. That woman was the teacher I needed to have in my life at that moment, and I will always be grateful for the lesson she taught me that day.

There have been many more teachers in my life, and each one has taught me just what I needed to learn at that time. Some of them have been people who loved me and were close to me, such as my grandmother. Others have been people who were difficult, rude, or angry but who nonetheless had something to teach me. But most of my teachers have been my life experiences. Each experience, whether happy or sad, comfortable or uncomfortable, tragic or joyous, has taught me something about myself I did not know before. Each one helped me to become a better person by forcing me to struggle, grow, change, or evolve. I believe we are here on this earth with one purpose—to grow to be like our Father. It is His intent to help us become the most like Him we possibly can, and the way He does this is by sending us the teachers that can transform our hearts.

CREATE THE HABITS

Learn What Truly Feeds You:

1. Think of an activity you did as a child that you absolutely loved. Is it something you might enjoy doing as an adult? If so, try doing it again and see if you still enjoy it as much as you did when you were young. If not, is there a more grown-up way to bring back that joy? For instance, if you loved playing with dolls as a child, perhaps you could start a vintage doll collection.

2. Try to fill the need for sweetness in your life with sweet experiences rather than with the food you eat. Are you craving ice cream? Maybe you could use a hug instead.

3. Listen to the wisdom of your body. Each sensation, craving, pain or symptom is your body's way

of telling you what it needs. Start paying close attention to the emotions, situations, and foods you eat or don't eat that coincide with your body's messages. Soon you will see patterns emerge, and you will know what it is your body is trying to tell you.

Try New Things:

1. Take a shot at a new activity you have always wanted to try but have resisted for whatever reason. Sign up for dance lessons or take a photography class. Don't expect to be perfect at it the first time you try it. Everyone has been a beginner at some point; don't pass judgment on yourself if you don't master it right away. Be willing to laugh when you feel like groaning.

2. If a friend invites you to try something you are not sure you will like, go for it. You may end up loving it, or you may hate it, but either way, you will have stepped out of your comfort zone and learned something along the way!

3. Learn how to prepare healthier versions of some of your favorite foods. Search online or in cookbooks for recipes that call for fresh, whole ingredients instead of pre-packaged, processed foods. Be willing to experiment with fruits and vegetables you have never tried before, or don't think you will like. Have fun with it and become a food aficionado!

Do More of What You Love:

1. Make a list of your soul feeders. What are those activities that are so enjoyable and natural for you they feel effortless? What things bring you the most joy and make you feel the most like yourself when you are doing them?
2. See how many of your soul feeders you can incorporate into your daily routine. If they can't be done daily, plan a time to do them as often as you possibly can. Give yourself permission to do the things you really love doing without feeling guilty about how much time it takes.
3. Schedule time each day for your own personal Sacred Time. This is your time to read uplifting books, meditate, pray, ponder, write in a gratitude journal, or take a walk in nature. Make it part of your daily routine, and make it non-negotiable.

Be on the Lookout For Your Teachers:

1. Be aware that each person, situation, and experience in your life is there for a reason. Ask yourself, "What am I supposed to learn from this?" instead of asking, "Why me?"
2. Be willing to learn from the wisdom and experience of others. We are not here to go it all alone—it is okay to ask for help when you need it. The next time you think you can figure it out for yourself,

ask someone with more experience to show you how. It will make their day.

Affirmations:

- I allow myself time each day to do those things that truly feed my soul. There is plenty of time to do what I love.
- I am a student of all that is good, beautiful and true. I take time each day for sacred study, pondering, and reflection.
- I am in sync with my body and I understand the messages and signals it sends me.
- I listen to the wisdom of my body.
- I am open to trying new things and I enjoy the process of learning.
- I choose to nourish my body with healthy foods that are prepared with love.
- When the student is ready, the teacher will appear. I am ready and willing to learn from all of the teachers who show up in my life.

Use this space to write your own learning habits and affirmations:

Habit # 3: Stillness

"And he arose, and rebuked the wind, and said unto the sea, 'Peace, be still.' And the wind ceased, and there was a great calm." Mark 4:39

Be Your Own Angel

Recently, I was having a quite horrible day. I had let myself become overwhelmed with the pressures of life and I felt as if I was barely keeping my head above water. There were financial pressures (putting two sons through college; buying an investment property that needed to be furnished and decorated); emotional pressures (becoming an empty nester; feeling isolated from family and friends); work pressures (helping my husband run a consulting business; writing my first book), and family pressures (becoming a grandma for the first time; worrying about my mom's health). I desperately wanted someone, anyone, to come to my rescue. I felt I needed support, and I needed it fast. My journal entry from that day reads, "*Today I am feeling submerged. I am drowning. I feel hopeless. I have no idea what I am doing. I am overwhelmed. So many major life events are coming up at the same time. My stomach is in knots. My knee is swollen and painful all the time. My body is screaming at me with headaches, fatigue, sleeplessness, inflammation, pain—all while I am trying to write a book about physical healing through spiritual habits! I can see the irony. I want to laugh about it, but right now I just feel like crying. I'm trying to do all I can to let go of this giant ball of stress inside of me, but it just seems to keep on growing. How do you stay relaxed while still functioning at your highest level? God, please show me what to do. I am asking for your help. I am totally useless without you.*"

After writing that journal entry, and still feeling distressed, I knelt down and asked God to send someone to support me that day. I just needed to know someone was out there who cared about me and was sympathetic to what I was going through. I had heard stories of others who had prayed for help and received it in the form of some earthly angel who felt prompted to stop by and say hello and deliver cookies or a kind word. I wanted, no, I needed, my own angel to come to my rescue. So, I asked for one.

A few hours later, I met my husband for lunch. I didn't tell him how stressed out and emotional I was feeling, mostly because I thought I would start to cry if I did. All morning

I had been trying to think of a catchy title for my book, so I ran my latest idea past him. He usually had great insights and feedback for me, so I was eager to hear what he thought of it.

"So, I'm thinking of calling it 'Holy Habits'", I said. "What do you think of that?"

He waved his hand back and forth in a gesture that implied it was just so-so. "I don't know," he replied, "it kind of makes me think about nuns." Then he moved on to some other subject, not even realizing how devastated I was at his lack of interest in my amazing, well-thought-out, best-selling book title.

"Well," I thought to myself, "apparently David is not going to be my earthly angel today."

As the day wore on, I kept waiting for my angel to appear. Would it be my next-door neighbor stopping by to chat and see how I was doing? Would it be a friend calling to see if I would like to go to lunch with her next week? Would it be a stranger who gave me an unexpected compliment or offered to buy my herbal tea at Starbucks? I didn't know, but I was excited to see who it would be and what sort of random act of kindness he or she had planned for me.

All day long I waited, but no angel. The funny thing is, I wasn't really surprised. Did I really think that God was going to send someone to cater to me just because I was having a rotten day? Not really. But, a small part of me had hoped that He would, because that would be such an easy way for me to feel better. That night as I lay quietly in bed reflecting on the day, it hit me. God had not abandoned me or forsaken me. True, He didn't send me the angel I had asked for, but that was because I didn't really need one. I knew deep down inside me that eventually everything would be okay, even if it didn't feel like it right now. There was a part of me that trusted not only in the belief that all would be well, but also in the knowledge that it already was. I had been looking for an angel, some outside source, to come and give me the support I thought I needed, but all the support I really needed had been there all along. In the stillness, I could feel it. I could feel Him, and I thought I heard Him say, "Linda, I love you, but sometimes you have to be your own angel."

***

"Stillness is the language God speaks –
everything else is just a bad translation."
-- Eckhart Tolle

The day I prayed for an angel to come and rescue me, I had been listening to a voice. The voice was coming from inside me, but it wasn't me. It was the voice in my head that never stopped talking, never stopped worrying, and never stopped analyzing. It was the same voice I had been listening to during all those years when I hated my body, my appearance, and myself. It was so easy to get caught up in listening to the voice that I forgot it wasn't the real me. I became mesmerized, hypnotized by the voice, and I accepted as truth everything it told me. I believe it is part of our human experience to have thoughts that don't serve us, that try to sabotage our best efforts to improve, learn, and progress. Part of the challenge of being human is learning to quiet this inner voice, or at least stop paying so much attention to it, and learning to listen instead to our higher selves, our own inner wisdom.

In his groundbreaking book "A New Earth," Eckhart Tolle describes a shift in consciousness that is beginning to take place in our world. This change begins with each one of us recognizing our true selves as the awareness behind our thoughts. He says, *"...at the heart of the new consciousness lies the transcendence of thought, the newfound ability of rising above thought, of realizing a dimension within yourself that is infinitely more vast than thought. You then no longer derive your identity, your sense of who you are, from the incessant stream of thinking that in the old consciousness you take to be yourself. What a liberation to realize that the 'voice in my head' is not who I am. Who am I then? The one who sees that. The awareness that is prior to thought, the space in which the thought—or the emotion or sense perception - happens."* (A New Earth, p. 21-22)

I wanted to rise above the voice—to move to that higher plane where I could discern thought from awareness.

But how? I wanted to stop identifying with the voice that told me I was drowning, hopeless, and overwhelmed, and instead give my attention to the peaceful awareness that came to me as I lay in my bed that night. How could I learn to tell the difference between the incessantly chattering voice in my head and my wise inner voice? I gave this a lot of thought, and eventually, I came to this conclusion: It is easy to distinguish between these two opposing voices because one of them is crazy and the other one is sane.

THE CRAZY VOICE:

- Is based in fear: *"What if this happens?" "What if that doesn't happen?"*
- Is overly dramatic: *"I am drowning." "I feel hopeless."*
- Is self-centered: *"I need someone to help me." "Why is this happening to me?"*
- Seeks to control: *"I have to do something about this." "I'm doing all I can, and it's not enough."*
- Is negative: *"Life is hard." "I can't do this anymore."*
- Jumps to conclusions: *"This is never going to work." "No one will ever accept me."*
- Is irrational: *"If I could just fall into a coma for a few weeks, I would feel better." "If I died right now, they'd all be sorry."*

THE SANE VOICE:

- Is based in love: *"How can I lift or support someone else?" "What can I do to help?"*
- Is reassuring: *"This is not going to kill me." "Everything is going to be all right."*
- Is generous: *"Everyone is doing the best they can." "He's probably having a hard day."*
- Is non-attached: *"God is in control, not me." "It is what it is."*
- Is positive: *"Life is good." "I can see this turning out so well."*
- Is hopeful: *"This is going to work." "Things will get better."*
- Is rational: *"This is a valuable lesson for me to be learning right now." "Sometimes life is hard, and that's okay."*

I could see the difference between these two opposing powers—the power of thought and the power of stillness, but it was still difficult to remember that the thoughts from the crazy voice were usually not true and rarely, if ever, helpful. Besides that, the crazy voice was much louder and more persistent than the sane voice, and it usually made its case much more forcefully than the sane voice did. How could I avoid getting caught up in the crazy voice when it's messages were so convincing and so much easier to believe? I decided I needed to make a plan. I had to find ways to silence or ignore my inner critic, and give more heed to my inner wisdom. I was sure I had been on the right track when I decided to pray for help, but instead of praying for angels to come to my rescue, perhaps I should have been praying for something else entirely.

* * *

"Be still and know that I am God." Proverbs 46:10

Be Still

In my prayer of desperation, I had asked God to send an angel to come to my rescue. But what did I need to be rescued from? Did I really require someone to come and save me? I wasn't in any actual physical danger. I wasn't bleeding or in pain. I wasn't really drowning or helpless or submerged. So what was I hoping to be rescued from? It was this: my own thoughts. The *thought* that I was drowning was torturing me, but I was not, in reality, drowning. The *thought* that I was helpless was filling me with doubt and fear, but I was not at all helpless. It was thinking about and dwelling upon all my concerns that was causing me to feel overwhelmed more than the actual concerns themselves. What I really needed help with was finding a peaceful place amongst all of the agitated thoughts that were tumbling around in my head. I knew it was not possible to remain in a constant state of tranquility and stillness, but I could practice being more still. It was not my intention to never experience worry, stress or anxiety about life. My goal was to worry less about worrying, stress less about stressing, and have less anxiety about feeling anxious. These are normal feelings we all experience from time to time, but I realized I did not have to get caught up in them or let them control me. I was ready to let go of the familiar feelings of stress, anxiety, worry, and guilt, and replace them with the calm, peaceful, stillness of God.

In his book, "The Untethered Soul," Michael A. Singer teaches that we need to stop telling our minds to fix everything we perceive to be wrong with our lives. He says, *"...stop telling your mind that its job is to fix your personal problems. This job has broken the mind and disturbed the entire psyche. It has created fear, anxiety, and neurosis. Your mind has very little control over this world. It is neither omniscient nor omnipotent. It cannot control the weather and other natural forces. Nor can it control all people, places, and things around you. You have given your mind an impossible task by asking it to manipulate the world in order to fix your personal inner problems. If you want to achieve a healthy state of being, stop asking your mind to do this. Just relieve your mind of the job of making sure that everyone and everything will be the way you need them to be so that you can feel better inside. Your mind is not qualified for that job. Fire it, and let go of your inner problems instead."*

He goes on to say, *"By watching your mind, you will notice that it is engaged in the process of trying to make everything okay. Consciously remember that this is not what you want to do, and then gently disengage. Do not fight it. Do not ever fight your mind. You will never win. It will either beat you now, or you will suppress it and it will come back and beat you later. Instead of fighting the mind, just don't participate in it. When you see the mind telling you how to fix the world and everyone in it in order to suit yourself, just don't listen."* (The Untethered Soul, P 94.)

When I read these words, I was inspired to give stillness a chance. I have always been a doer, making sure all the work was done before I could relax and enjoy life, and it seemed like stress was what kept me going. But the more I learned about stress and it's effects on the body, I knew I needed to do something different. Studies have found there are a myriad of health problems related to stress. Stress has been shown to worsen or increase the risk of conditions like obesity, heart disease, asthma, depression, diabetes, Alzheimer's disease, and gastrointestinal problems, just to name a few. This proves to me that stress is not just in our heads. It is the body's physical reaction to a perceived danger—also known as the fight-or-flight response. When we feel threatened, either by an actual outside force or by an imagined one, our blood vessels constrict, blood pressure and pulse rates increase, breathing becomes faster and more shallow, and our bloodstreams are flooded with hormones like adrenaline and cortisol, also known as the stress hormones. If not kept in check, all of these physical reactions in the body can, over time, lead to serious and life threatening health problems.

In my quest to live a healthier life, I definitely needed to reduce my stress levels and find a way to live in a more peaceful and calm manner. I recalled the scripture found in Matthew 6:28-30: *"Consider the lilies of the field, how they grow; they toil not, neither do they spin: And yet I say unto you, That even Solomon in all his glory was not arrayed like one of these. Wherefore, if God so clothe the grass of the field, which to day is, and to morrow is cast into the oven, shall he not much more clothe you, O ye of little faith?"*

I could see that for all of my toiling and spinning, all of my working and worrying, I was not making a lot of progress. As I said in my journal entry, I was –submerged—trying to do it all on my own was not working. I was drowning and hopeless—listening to the crazy voice in my head was not helping. I was –overwhelmed—running around in a state of stress and anxiety was not making me more efficient, and my body was starting to send me desperate messages that something was wrong—headaches, knee pain, fatigue, etc. It was finally time to stop talking about stillness and start putting it into practice.

* * *

One very important concept I learned in my training as a health coach is that if a food doesn't taste good to you, you probably don't need it. If you hate the taste of broccoli, you should not force yourself to eat a plateful of it. Eating food you despise will not do your body any good and will not produce any health benefits. I believe the same goes for exercise. It will not benefit your body to do a workout you hate doing. You can force yourself to go to spin class, but if you absolutely loathe every moment of being there, you might as well have stayed home and sat on the sofa. I'm not saying you should not push your body or work it hard enough to sweat and get good and tired, but forcing your body to do something it hates will not produce good health. Exercising because you hate your body and pushing it to the limits as a form of punishment will not promote wellness. No good change ever comes from hate. Your body knows what it needs and what it doesn't, and one of the ways it will communicate those needs is through likes and dislikes. So, even though I liked the idea of meditation, I had a hard time actually sitting down and putting it into practice. Meditating felt like just one more thing I should do because I knew it was good for me, but when it came time to do it, it was like a huge plate of broccoli staring me in the face.

It is also true, however, that we can develop a love for broccoli by combining it with some other food that we love, such as cheese or even chocolate. We can develop a love for riding a stationary bike if we combine it with something we are passionate about, such as classical music. I have even heard of punk rock yoga classes becoming popular lately. Just because something is traditionally done a certain way does not mean we can't tweak it so that it better assimilates with our lives, our personalities, and our preferences. That was what I needed to do with meditation. I knew I needed to practice stillness on a regular basis in order to rise above the chaos and chatter in my mind, but it had to be done in a way that made sense for me.

Meditation is traditionally, *"a practice in which an individual trains the mind or induces a mode of consciousness either to realize some benefit, or as an end in itself."* (Wikipedia – Meditation) From what I read about meditation, I understood that it was a practice of sitting quietly while focusing on my breathing or on the sensations in my body, observing and being aware of my thoughts, and being in a relaxed state. However, sitting down for twenty or thirty minutes at a time in complete silence was unnerving and uncomfortable. I didn't enjoy it or look forward to doing it. I felt that gritting my teeth and holding still for a period of time was not my idea of relaxation, and I'm pretty sure it wasn't what the ancient teachers of meditation practices had in mind either. If the idea of a meditation practice was to calm the mind, to reboot the computer, so to speak, then it needed to feel like a calming, pleasant, happy experience. Otherwise, I was just plugging my nose and gulping down my broccoli, which I knew did no good whatsoever.

I started looking for ways to meditate that sounded enjoyable to me. One of my first attempts at meditating was joining an online 21-day meditation challenge. I loved the idea of spending peaceful mornings in silence and introspection, and ending my day with another serene and blissful experience. I think I may have made it five or six days before giving up. I just was not ready to incorporate such a lofty challenge into my daily life. Next, I bought a book about meditation and attempted to follow the instructions for an 8-week program that promised to help me "discover deep wellsprings of peace and contentment" within myself. I made it a little farther this time, arriving at week two before my enthusiasm began to dwindle and eventually faded away until I was back at square one. Although I did learn a lot from these attempts at developing a daily meditation practice, I still felt I had not found the appropriate one for me.

Then one day I came across a magazine article that suggested any activity could become a meditation if we simply bring awareness to it. For one woman featured in the article, dancing was a meditation. When she danced, her mind was free from stressful thoughts and worry. For another man featured in the article, sculpting was a form of meditation. When he was creating a beautiful work of art, everything else seemed to fall away and his mind was clear, focused, and relaxed. For another man, playing a familiar piece of music on the piano was his meditation. When his fingers united with the keys, he entered into a state of pure bliss and contentment. It was just as Albert Einstein and Mihaly Csikszentmihalyi had taught—these people had found a way to enter into "the flow", that place of enjoyment and bliss where we don't even notice the passing of time. They were absorbed in something they loved, something they were familiar with, and something they were good at. The activities were also somewhat repetitive, which helped the mind to relax and return to its natural state of ease and bliss.

When I was about ten or eleven years old, I was in the Merry Miss Sunday school class. I remember our teacher, a nice little old lady who wanted to teach us girls skills that she considered useful. I don't recall her name anymore, but I will never forget what she taught me. I learned how to create washcloths, potholders, granny squares, and doll blankets out of a skein of yarn and a metal hook. Since I learned to crochet at such a young age, it always stuck with me and came easily to me. I enjoyed creating my hand-made works of art for many years, but I never connected that process to stillness or peace of mind. I could see now that it was. The process was creative, focused, repetitive, and relaxing. It was a meditation. I didn't need to sit cross-legged in a quiet room with my palms up and my eyes closed unless I really wanted to (most of the time, I didn't). My meditation practice could be as simple as picking up some yarn and a hook and crocheting my way to inner peace.

It also has been suggested that many everyday activities could be an opportunity to practice awareness and stillness. Certain routine undertakings can be used as a trigger to remind us to be still, release tension and stress, and simply observe our thoughts. Everyday tasks such as brushing your teeth, washing dishes, folding laundry, taking out the trash, or driving to work can, with a little practice, be small moments of meditation throughout the day. Instead of hurrying through the task as quickly as possible, it is much more enjoyable and relaxing to do it deliberately and with a lot of love. As I began to try to incorporate these small meditative moments into my daily life, I really appreciated the simplicity of it. Meditation did not have to be a major production or take any extra time. Bringing awareness to tasks I was already doing was an easy way to relax my mind and allow my inner peace to rise to the surface once again. Just as wellness and good health are the natural state of the body and the set point that it always strives to return to, I believe that stillness, bliss and peace are the natural state of the mind. If given the chance, the mind will return to that state where it is most tranquil and balanced.

* * *

"If you have a bad thought about yourself, tell it to go to hell, because that is exactly where it came from." - Brigham Young

"B.U.M.P." It Up

One thing I noticed as I attempted to add moments of meditation to my day was that the crazy voice in my head didn't like it very much. The more earnest I was at trying to still my mind and ignore the voice, the louder the voice seemed to become. The more I worked on listening to my inner wisdom, the more the crazy voice would come forward with negative thoughts to disturb my peace. How could I find a way to push past the resistance I was experiencing? I found four tools that have been extremely helpful in my quest for a calmer mind. These four tools have helped me to "B.U.M.P." up my ability to practice stillness in my everyday life.

> B – Breathe
> U – Unplug From Negative Thoughts
> M – Repeat a Mantra
> P – Pray

1. Breathe: In his book, "Natural Health, Natural Medicine", Dr. Andrew Weil shares a simple way to shift our awareness whenever we find ourselves consumed by negative or defeating thoughts. He calls it *"conscious regulation of breath."* It is a simple breathing exercise that can be done at any time or any place that you may be in. Although the exercise can be done in any position, Dr. Weil recommends doing it in a seated position with your back straight. Place the tip of your tongue against the gum tissue just behind your front teeth and hold it there throughout the exercise.

First, exhale completely through the mouth.

- Close your mouth and inhale through the nose as you slowly count to four.
- Hold your breath for a count of seven.
- Exhale completely through the mouth for a count of eight.
- Inhale again and repeat the cycle three more times for a total of four breath cycles.

It is Dr. Weil's assertion that this exercise is a natural tranquilizer for the nervous system. It brings about an immediate shift in consciousness and neutralizes stress. He recommends practicing this breathing technique at least twice a day, or as often as needed. I have found it helpful in relaxing my mind in preparation for going to sleep at night, before undertaking a task that requires focus and concentration, or in any stressful or upsetting situation. When we experience stress, our breathing becomes shallow, our pulse rate quickens, our pupils dilate, and our blood pressure increases. Remembering to practice this simple technique during times of stress can be very useful in calming the body and returning the mind to a state of stillness.

2. Unplug from negative thoughts: When we are caught up in the chatter of our minds, we rarely

see our thoughts for what they really are—just thoughts. They are not real; they are merely ideas our mind is creating. Most of the time, we are lost in thoughts about something that has happened to us in the past—"I can't believe she actually said that to me", or something we anticipate happening in the future—"He is probably going to let me down again." Each of us also has little tracks we play over and over again in our minds without even being aware of it—"I need to lose weight," or "I never win." But if we can recognize these thought patterns, it is easier to unplug from them, to take a step back and see them for what they are. The mind is like a computer that stores all the data or thoughts that we generate. By making judgments, being critical, and repeating patterns, the mind is attempting to categorize and make sense of all that is going on around and inside of us. Once we recognize our mind is only trying to be helpful by generating these thought patterns, we can view ourselves and the crazy voice in our minds with compassion and gratitude. There is no need to fight or argue with our thoughts. We can instead say, "Thank you, but that is not helpful. I release my attachment to you." Or, in a case where the thoughts are particularly offensive, just do as Brigham Young suggested and tell them to go to hell.

3. Repeat a mantra: Loving kindness meditation is a form of meditation where you silently repeat

certain phrases that invoke love or kind feelings towards others. This same concept can also be used to invoke kind and loving feelings towards ourselves. When you find yourself repeating limiting thoughts about yourself, replace them with a positive, loving affirmation or mantra. For example, instead of telling yourself, "I'm never going to be happy", repeat in your mind, "I choose to be happy now." Instead of saying, "I don't have time to do all that I need to do", say, "There is plenty of time. Everything that needs to get done will be done." When I first started writing this book, I kept telling myself that writing a book was hard. Once I realized what I was doing, I changed what I was telling myself. I started to repeat in my mind, "Writing a book is easy. It is such a joyful experience to be writing my first book." After that, the work became much more enjoyable and ideas began to flow effortlessly.

4. Pray: Prayer is an excellent form of meditation that can be practiced at any time. Keeping a silent prayer in our hearts can be a wonderful way to bring more peace and contentment into our daily lives. The day I prayed for an angel to come to my rescue, I didn't realize the help I was so desperately seeking was already there, I just couldn't see it because I was so caught up in my thoughts. I was engulfed by the fear my thoughts were creating. Instead of praying for help in the form of an angel, I should have prayed for love. I didn't even need to

ask for love to come to me, because it is the natural state of our existence. Love is always available to us if we just remember it. Love is the opposite of fear and in order to overcome my fear, I needed to go to the actual source of love itself. God is love. Perfect love casts out fear. Love conquers all. Prayer is not a way for us to pick up the phone and order what we want, or what we, in our finite understanding, think we need. Prayer is God's way of bringing us into alignment with what he knows is best for us. He knows what we need before we even ask, and He will run to answer our cries, just not always in the way we expect. When we pray, we gain access to an unlimited source of love, peace, and joy.

* * *

CREATE THE HABITS

Be Your Own Angel:

1. Learn to tell the difference between the crazy, irrational voice in your head and the sane, loving voice that is the real you. Pay attention to the thoughts that run through your mind throughout the day. Realize any fearful, negative, or self-centered thoughts are the crazy voice, and only the loving, positive, and hopeful thoughts are true.

Practice bringing your focus and attention to your own inner wisdom.

2. Relieve your mind of the burden of having to solve all of your problems. Take a step back from the thoughts that seek to control and see them for what they are—destructive and useless. Remember that the "real" you is not the chattering, thinking mind, but the awareness that you are thinking. Relax into that awareness and allow your higher self to step forward.

3. Stop using stress as a tool for getting things done. Turn instead to your inner wisdom and consider how you can accomplish more by "doing" less. The lilies of the field toil not, neither do they spin. Where in your life can you release the urge to toil and spin?

Be Still:

1. Find a way of practicing stillness that works for you. Try combining meditation with an activity you enjoy and know how to do well, such as dancing, playing a musical instrument, sewing, or creating art. Bring your full attention to the task and relax into the bliss of the moment.

2. Use routine daily tasks as a trigger to remind yourself to practice stillness. Incorporating small "meditative moments" throughout your day will help your mind return to its natural state of peace and joy.

B.U.M.P. It Up:

1. Breathe: Practice Dr. Weil's 4-7-8 breathing technique whenever you are in a stressful situation and need to calm your mind. Try doing it before going to bed at night to help you fall asleep faster and sleep more soundly.

2. Unplug: Recognize your negative thought patterns and notice when you are caught up in thoughts of the past, or of things that may or may not happen in the future. Bring your focus back to the present and thank your mind for trying to be helpful. Then release attachment to those thoughts.

3. Repeat a Mantra: Replace negative repeating thoughts with positive, loving mantras. Instead of thinking, "I'm such a loser", repeat in your mind or aloud, "Good things are always happening to me". Each time you notice a negative thought, replace it with kind, uplifting words that build up instead of tear down.

4. Pray: When you are feeling overwhelmed or stressed out, say a silent prayer that you will have access to God's unlimited source of love and peace. Remember that you don't always need someone to come to your rescue—your own inner joy and tranquility are always present and can be accessed at any time.

Affirmations:

- I allow time each day for stillness, gratitude, and reflection.
- I am a calm and peaceful influence on all those around me.
- I trust my own inner wisdom and the stillness that is always within me.
- I am the awareness behind my thoughts. My thoughts are not me.
- I choose to release all thoughts of anxiety, stress, and worry.
- Stillness, bliss, and peace are the natural state of my mind.

Use this space to write your own stillness habits and affirmations:

Habit # 4: Humility

"...he remembereth them, he forgetteth not the cry of the humble." Psalms 9:12

Ask God For Help

There have been two times in my life when I received an immediate answer to a prayer. The first happened when I was fifteen years old and was away at girl's camp. I was having a great time being in nature, visiting with my friends, and enjoying all the camp activities. On the second day of camp, my sister unexpectedly arrived and informed me I needed to go home with her because our grandmother had passed away. I grew up next door to my grandma, and she was like a second mother to me. I knew if I went home, I would have to face the reality she was gone and deal with my grief, so I told my sister I would not go. A wise leader learned of the situation, and told my sister and me to go into her tent, kneel down in prayer, and ask God what we should do. Since neither of us was comfortable praying aloud, my sister and I each said our own prayer. As I stood up from saying my prayer, I no longer had any desire to stay at the camp. I wanted to go home and be with my family. My feelings had completely changed, and I knew my prayer had been answered.

The second experience happened when I was dating my husband. We had been going out for about a year and had started talking seriously about marriage. I was nervous about making such a huge commitment at only nineteen years of age, so I took the matter to God. I poured out my feelings to Him; told Him I had decided David was a good man, that I loved him, and that unless I was directed otherwise, I was going to marry him. Immediately upon standing up from that prayer, I knew David was the right person for me to spend my life with. I felt a warm and peaceful assurance that I had made the right decision. Because of these two instances in my life, I have always believed in the power of prayer. I knew not every prayer received such an immediate answer, but I trusted God would always answer my prayers in a way that was best for me. Until a few years ago, however, one thing I had never considered praying about or asking God to help me with was my physical wellness. Sure, I had prayed for health and strength, a general reference to my physical well-being, but I had never prayed to know how to care for my body, how to interpret the messages it was sending me, or for the desire to take better care of it.

I learned this concept when I was in training to become a certified health coach. In one of my weekly calls with my own personal health coach, I expressed to her my frustration at not enjoying exercise. "I hate going to the gym," I said. "I just don't like being there, so I don't go." Then Jane, my coach, asked me a series of questions I will never forget: "You said you believe in God, right?" "Yes," I replied. "And you pray to Him when you need help?" "Yes, I do." "Then have you ever considered praying for Him to help you *want* to exercise?" I was speechless. I couldn't believe that in all of my life, I had never even considered the fact that God could and would help me overcome anything—including my lack of desire to exercise! If anyone cared about my body more than I did, it was the One who had created it and given it to me.

Taking Jane's advice, I turned to God for guidance about how to give my body the movement and exercise it needed and craved. I want to point out that I did not ask for God to make me suddenly love going to the gym—I was pretty sure that was never going to happen. Rather, I prayed to know how best to give my body the movement and exercise it was in need of, and for the desire to make it a daily practice. Slowly, I came to understand I needed to let go of my preconceived notions of what "exercise" consisted of. I had always believed that in order to work out, I had to go to a gym or a formal exercise class or it didn't really count. Once I let go of that notion, I was free to do what my body enjoyed and responded to. Going for a walk in the late afternoon with my husband and our little dog became a daily routine that energized and invigorated me. Doing some yoga stretches for about thirty minutes at the end of each day helped keep my muscles strong and flexible. I also found that doing it before bedtime worked well for me because it helped me sleep better. By turning to my Creator for guidance in caring for my body and paying attention to the signals my body was sending me, I was able to find a routine that felt right and worked for me.

Linda, the mother of a friend of mine, shared with me a similar experience that she had. She related to me that several years ago, when she was in her late forties she went on a trip with her family to some sites on a pioneer trail and various places in the Dakotas. While walking on a path with a slight incline at one of the sites, she started to feel winded and quite unwell. She sat down on a bench along the trail and told the rest of her family to go on without her. Throughout the rest of the trip she would often sit and wait while the others walked the trails. She was afraid to join them because she thought she might have a heart attack. Once back at home, Linda was surprised to find that she weighed twenty-five pounds more than she had originally thought.

Determined to lose the weight and regain her energy, she tried many different diet and exercise plans, but none of them brought her the lasting results she desired. Finally, not knowing what else to do, she took the matter to God. She fervently prayed to know how to care for her body, lose the excess weight, and feel healthier and happier. She felt inspired to begin walking regularly, cook healthier meals for her family, and be more careful about the foods she took into her body. Over the next year, she lost sixty pounds. By being humble enough to turn to God for help and direction, Linda received the inspiration she had been searching for, and over time was able to lose weight and dramatically improve her health.

Not unlike many others, I had long held the belief that exercising and taking care of my body required willpower, and each time I fell short I felt like a failure. But maintaining our health is not about willpower, it's about *His* power! If we rely on our own strength, on our own willpower, we will not get very far. Cravings set in. We lose momentum. We get bored. We give up. The body is always going to win in a battle of wills. But by relying on His power and strength, we can do all things. If we humbly turn to God in our weakened state and ask for His help, guidance, love and power to be applied in our lives, we will not fail. He will inspire our minds and show us what we need to do in order to care for the magnificent gift he gave to us, and as we follow his guidance, we will continue to grow in health and wisdom.

> *"Humility is not thinking less of yourself,*
> *it is thinking of yourself less." -- C.S. Lewis*

See the Needs of Others

We've all heard the saying, "In order to lift someone else, you must be standing on higher ground." I have thought about that a lot, and I don't believe it to be true. I think the only requirement to be able to lift somebody is to notice that they have stumbled. None of us is really on higher ground than anyone else; we are all just at different points on the journey. But it is easy to forget to look outward and see what is going on around us when we are so intently focused on the struggles and challenges of our own lives. We can become so wrapped up in our own business that we neglect to look outward and notice the needs of others. How often are we so consumed with thoughts of ourselves, what *we* are suffering, what *we* are worried about, what *we* are going through, that we fail to notice a fellow traveler has stumbled?

In the movie, "The Help", Hilly's mother loves watching soap operas on her little black and white portable TV. She calls it "watching her stories." All around her, all kinds of real life drama is playing out, but she is so busy watching her "stories" that she doesn't even notice. How often do we do the same? How often are we so consumed by the stories playing in our own head that we miss the real life stories playing out all around us? I have heard it suggested we are better able to recognize the suffering of others and respond appropriately to their needs when we ourselves are experiencing the same or a similar challenge. Being able to turn outward and serve when our instinct is to focus inward and be self-absorbed is the mark of true humility.

The health benefits of turning our thoughts outward and doing good to others have been scientifically documented. Several studies over the past twenty years have shown that regularly giving service to others is associated with increased immunity, tolerance for pain, social trust, tranquility, confidence and self-esteem. Serving and volunteering is also associated with decreased depression and mortality rates. When we have meaningful interactions with others in the form of eye-to-eye contact, touching, and smiling, the body releases a hormone called oxytocin, which helps cells repair themselves, store nutrients, and grow. Oxytocin also helps us bond with those around us and handle stress better. I learned of these benefits firsthand when I had the opportunity several years ago to take care of my mother after an accident.

In 2001, my mom slipped and fell while shampooing her carpets and broke her back and her wrist. Even though I had three boys at home to take care of, I was able to go and stay with my mom for a week and help her recover. She was unable to walk, sit up, go to the bathroom, eat, or do anything without my assistance. I didn't have time to worry about anything other than taking care of her. At one point, it took me an hour just to get her positioned from lying down to sitting up in bed. This was a horrible and painful ordeal for my mother, but it was also a great bonding experience for us. As I put my own needs aside and focused on her care, I learned to truly appreciate her and all she had done for me throughout my life. For years, she had taken care of me, fed me, clothed me, and nurtured me, and now it was my turn to return that loving service. For that one week, I forgot myself and served someone I loved. My own needs became secondary, and I was no longer focused on every little ache and pain that might be going on in my own body. It was a very healing experience to let go of that for a time. Of course, I would not have wished for this accident to happen, but I was extremely grateful and humbled to be able to provide the help my mom needed at that time.

During a recent severe windstorm in our area, a large tree in our backyard was blown over. The tree, which was very close to our house, fell onto our hot tub doing some minor damage. I was home alone at the time and didn't even hear the tree fall because the wind was howling so loudly. I could hear people talking outside but it wasn't until my husband, who had just arrived at our home, called me from the back yard that I realized what had happened. A few of our neighbors, some of whom had uprooted trees in their own yards to deal with, had shown up in the dark of night with hacksaws and spotlights to help remove the damaged tree. They took the time to help us out even though they had damage in their own yards that needed their attention. This was an example to me of how we can turn our focus outward and notice the needs of others even in the midst of our own trials.

Having a continual inward mental focus is like a disease that keeps us from living a full, rich, healthy life. How can we feel completely alive, vibrant, and engaged with life if we are continually focused on what is going on in our heads? By turning our thoughts outward and noticing when others may need us, we escape the drama of our own stories, and we are then better able to reach out to lift someone who has stumbled on the path. As we lift and support others, we are able to forget our own little problems for a while, and we feel better both mentally and physically as a result.

"Life is a long lesson in humility." -- *Sir James Matthew Barrie*

Accept Help From Others

I will never forget an incident that happened a few years ago when my mom and sister came for a visit. One of our favorite activities to do together is shopping, so we decided to go to the mall for the afternoon. After arriving at the mall, my little British mama realized it was teatime, so we stopped at a fast food restaurant in the food court to get her a cup of hot, black tea. As we sat down at our table, my mom accidentally knocked over the boiling hot tea and it spilled onto the table and all over her legs.

Luckily, there happened to be a nurse sitting at the table next to us who saw what had happened. She immediately sprang into action. She whisked my mom into the employee bathroom, while ordering the workers to prepare some cold compresses with rags and ice. Once in the bathroom, she helped my mom remove her pants so the scalding hot water would not continue to burn her legs. Then she applied the cold compresses to her skin to prevent any further damage. My mom ended up with minor burns on her legs that could have been much worse if this stranger had not taken immediate action.

What amazed me most about this lady is that she noticed right away someone needed her assistance and took action. She didn't wait to see if someone else stepped forward to help or ask if there was anything she could do. I suppose her training as a nurse kicked in and she went into action mode. She saw a need and quickly jumped in to be of service. She didn't wait, didn't hesitate, didn't ignore. She cared. She loved. She helped.

If this woman had been absorbed in her thoughts, or "off in her own little world", she may not have been aware anything had happened and that someone needed help only she could give at that moment. I also admire my mom for being humble enough to accept help from a total stranger. Stripping down to your undies in a public bathroom in front of someone you have never met is a rather embarrassing and humbling experience, to say the least. I thought about how many times I had refused to accept help from someone because I was too proud. Often I had insisted on figuring things out on my own rather than asking for assistance from someone with more experience or knowledge. How could I be more like my mom and be willing to accept help when I needed it?

I remember one experience that humbled me and taught me to accept the help of others rather than always believing I am on my own. I was attending a girl's camp again, this time as a leader, and one of our activities was a rope course. The course was set up on a hillside with lots of trees, bushes and rocks that would serve as obstacles. As leaders, we were able to participate in the activity in advance so we would know how to assist those who were running the event for the girls later in the day.

Each of us was blindfolded and handed a raw egg, which represented a woman's virtue. We were told to safeguard the egg, and that under no circumstance should we allow the egg to become cracked, broken, or lost. The goal was to protect the egg at all costs. We were instructed there would be many challenges that would make it difficult to keep our egg safe, including thieves, tempters, trickery, and the difficult terrain the course was constructed on. But, we were told we could ask for help at any point. If we ever felt we needed assistance, we could simply raise our hand and someone would come to our aid. Well, apparently that very vital instruction did not register in my brain, because I struggled through the entire course with the belief that I was on my own.

Blindfolded, I stumbled over rocks and sagebrush, grasping the rope with one hand while cradling my egg in the other. After what seemed like hours of wandering in the darkness, I finally made it to the finish line with my egg; thankfully, still intact. Slightly scratched, disoriented and still blindfolded, I was guided to a grassy area where I was told to sit quietly and wait for further instructions. Once all the other leaders completed the course, we removed our blindfolds and discussed what we had learned. The course leader reminded us of the instructions we had been given at the beginning of the challenge, and many of us were surprised to hear we had been told we could raise our hand and ask for help. We had simply not been in a frame of mind that allowed us to be open and willing to accept help from another. We were in survival mode, convinced we had to make it through the course completely on our own. How much easier our journey would have been if we had paid attention to the help that was available all around us! All we had to do was ask.

Being humble and willing to ask for help does not come naturally to most of us. It takes a conscious effort to recognize we have access to help and assistance at any time if we are only willing to ask for it. It can be hard at times to admit that someone else has more knowledge than we do or more experience with a particular task or skill. It can be scary to reach out, be vulnerable, and ask for guidance, direction, or even just an extra set of helping hands. None of us has all the answers. Every one of us needs help from our fellow travelers from time to time. When we can see beyond our own "stories" and are willing to ask for and give assistance when the need arises, we begin to understand the true meaning of humility.

> *"If you are humble, nothing will touch you, neither praise nor disgrace, because you know what you are."*
> *-- Mother Teresa*

Go Deeper

When I think of a prideful person, I think of someone who wants to look good in the eyes of others but has no interest in actually doing or being good. The motives of a proud person are shallow, having only to do with what others can see from the outside.

When it comes to humility and health, I think a prideful person wants to *look* healthy more than he wants to actually *be* healthy. If he has to do unhealthy things in order to *appear* to be healthy on the outside, then so be it. The only thing that matters is how he looks, and what he had to do to look like that is insignificant. Just as a contestant on the TV show, "Survivor", will lie, cheat and steal in order to win the game, we often cheat our bodies out of proper nutrition, rest, and love in order to get them to look the way we think they should look. The problem with this type of thinking is that, obviously, it is not sustainable. The person who takes up smoking in order to lose weight and "look" healthy will eventually suffer the side effects of that habit: high blood pressure, osteoporosis, ulcers, poor circulation, premature wrinkling of the skin, lower libido and fertility, reduced lung capacity, and being thirty times more likely to have cancer than a non-smoker. A person who nibbles on nuts and candy throughout the day instead of eating regular meals in order to appear "healthy" and thin will eventually suffer the effects of malnutrition: muscle deterioration, fatigue, dizziness, sallow skin, hair loss, depression, bone and joint pain, and higher susceptibility to infections. Being thin does not equal being healthy. If it did, there would be no thin people with cancer, heart problems, or other diseases. Looking good on the outside in the short term is no replacement for feeling good inside and out over the long term.

When our hearts are humble, we do not concern ourselves with what we look like in the eyes of others. That does not mean we disregard our appearance or that we don't try to take care of our bodies the very best way we possibly can. It does mean that we feel no desire to appear one way on the outside while being something totally different on the inside. It also means we avoid comparing ourselves to anyone else because we realize that no one is inherently better or worse than another. We are all the same. Every one of us has both weaknesses and strengths. Being humble is knowing that not only are we not superior to anyone else, but we are not inferior either. All of us are alike before God, and true humility is recognizing that fact.

British writer G.K Chesterton wrote, *"How much larger your life would be if your self could become smaller in it; If you could really look at other men with common curiosity and pleasure... You would break out of this tiny and tawdry theatre in which your own little plot is always being played, and you would find yourself under a freer sky, and in a street full of splendid strangers."* When we see everyone around us with love and compassion, remembering we are no better and no worse, we are truly free. Free from comparison, envy and judgment. Free from a feeling of being separate from others. Free to be our authentic selves. That is how humility heals us, just as Mother Teresa said, we are not affected by praise or disgrace, because we know who we are. And when we know who we are, and extend that thought beyond ourselves to others, we *"walk in a street full of splendid strangers."*

The story is told of a wealthy businessman who ran out of gas on the side of the highway. Soon a passing car filled with four rather rough looking young men stopped to offer assistance. As the boys climbed from the car, the man was taken back by their appearance—all were dressed in black from head to toe, one wore a nose ring, another a Mohawk, and all of them were accessorized with many chains. As they walked toward the man, he thought to himself, "I'm going to die! These guys are going to kill me!"

The boys asked if the man was having car trouble, and he replied that he had run out of gas. "We can take you to a gas station," one of the boys told him. Reluctantly the man went with them, retrieved the needed gas, and was returned to his car unharmed. As the boys wished him well, waved good-bye, and drove away, the man felt ashamed for how he had reacted. These four young men did not appear at first glance to be the kind of people who would stop and offer assistance out of the goodness of their hearts. They did not fit the image in the man's mind of a Good Samaritan. He realized he had made an assumption based on the outward appearance of the boys, and he prayed that he could learn to have the kind of charity those young men had shown to him that day.

As I think back now on all those years I spent hating my body and wishing for it to be different, to be somehow better than it was, I realize I was being prideful. I was judging my body for how it appeared on the outside and determined it was not good enough. When we are filled with pride, we want things the way we want them. When we are humble, we accept things as they really are. I wanted my body to look different. I had a preconceived notion of what I wanted it to be, and it didn't fit the mold. So instead of lovingly working to make a change for the better, I wasted time and energy trying to make my body be something it wasn't. I didn't see it for the amazing gift it really was. I was no different from the man who assumed four harsh looking boys would never stop to help a clean-cut, well-dressed man in his hour of need. By judging myself, I was guilty of a lack of humility. Each time I looked in the mirror and made a negative comment about my appearance, each time I rejected a compliment from another, each and every time I criticized myself instead of expressing gratitude, I was guilty of pride.

Humility is not beating ourselves up, tearing ourselves down, or thinking ourselves less than anyone else. I was taking a very shallow view by basing my worth on what I looked like on the outside. I thought I was being humble by not loving and accepting myself as I was. Instead, I was practicing pride. I was being a jerk. Only a jerk would expect you to be something other than what you are, but that was exactly what I was doing to my body. I wasn't paying any attention to all the things that were right about me; I was mainly concerned with everything I judged to be wrong, lacking, and unacceptable. When I went deeper and started practicing gratitude instead of faultfinding, I finally began to heal.

CREATE THE HABITS

Ask God for Help:

1. Ask God, the Universe, or whatever your higher power is, to help you know how best to care for your body. Prayerfully ponder and meditate about what exercise is best for you, what foods will offer the most nutrition and healing, how much rest it needs, etc. Ask for your heart to be filled with a desire to make these things a part of your daily routine.

2. Ask for help in interpreting the messages and signals from your body. Pay closer attention to cravings, changes in mood, energy levels and thought patterns, and pray for the inspiration to know what to do in response to those messages.

3. If there is some part of your body you currently dislike or even hate, ask God to help you come to love and appreciate that specific part of yourself. Ask for the desire to nurture, nourish, and care for this amazing gift in the very best ways possible.

See the Needs of Others:

1. Practice turning your focus outward instead of always focusing on your own "stories." When you are consumed with a particular challenge or

problem, look for someone who may be suffering in a similar way and reach out to them.

2. Watch for occasions to give service and offer assistance to those around you. When you leave your house each day, have the thought that there is someone who needs you, then look for that person as you go throughout the day.

Accept Help from Others:

1. For one entire day, practice accepting help graciously when it is offered. Say yes to the bag boy who offers to take your groceries to your car. If a stranger opens a door for you, smile and say thank you. Notice how many times a day people are there to help and serve you.

2. Be willing to ask for help from someone who has more experience, skill, or expertise than you currently do. Give up the need to do everything on your own and be humble enough to ask for assistance when you need it.

Go Deeper:

1. Evaluate your motives for wanting to exercise and/ or lose weight. Do you have a preconceived notion of what your body should look like? Do you want your body to function properly and have energy? If you need to, shift your focus from what your body

looks like on the outside to how it feels and what it needs in order to function at its highest level.

2. Try sending out love to everyone you meet and viewing them with "common curiosity and pleasure." Practice sincerely wishing blessings upon your fellow travelers in this earthly journey, knowing that even though we each have unique attributes and experiences, we are all alike before God.

3. Notice how many times a day you criticize yourself or your body. Is there a way you can start showing love to that part of you in order to help it begin to heal?

Affirmations:

- My comfort and my self-esteem come from God, and not from other people.
- I am of infinite worth and have a great purpose to fulfill on the earth.
- My inner beauty matters more to me than how I look on the outside.
- I am willing to ask for help when I need it.
- I am neither superior nor inferior to anyone. All are alike before God.
- My body is an amazing gift from God and He will show me how to care for this gift in the best ways possible.
- I am able to recognize the needs of others and offer my support whenever I can.

Use this space to write your own humility habits and affirmations:

Habit #5:
Surrender

"And the Lord, he it is that doth go before thee; he will be with thee, he will not fail thee, neither forsake thee; fear not, neither be dismayed." Deuteronomy 31:8

Let Go of Fear

The panic episodes usually happened in the middle of the night. I refer to them as "episodes" rather than "attacks" because the word attack implies I am a victim of some outside force and have no control over it. I would awaken with my heart pounding, my body trembling, and my breathing shallow and rapid. I would be consumed by an overwhelming sense of doom or dread, as if something horrible were going to happen at any moment. Logically, I knew that I was fine. I wasn't going to die and nothing terrible was actually going to happen. But I couldn't get my logical brain to convince my panic stricken mind to settle down. I came to expect these anxiety-ridden events on a nightly basis. It was almost as if my body had developed a pattern of going into panic mode, waking me like an evil alarm clock every morning at two a.m.

When the physical body sends us a signal of pain, it is telling us something is wrong and we need to take care of it. If we put our hand on a hot stove or smash our thumb with a hammer, for example, we feel pain and immediately act to remedy the injury. In a similar way, when the mind sends us the signal of fear, it is telling us that something is not right and needs to be addressed. Unfortunately, most of the time we do not react quickly in response to emotional pain signals. If we ignore pain signals from the body, the condition can worsen and cause serious illness or injury. If we ignore fear signals from the mind, the condition can likewise worsen and cause even more problems in the future. All emotional pain is based in fear.

The fact that I was having panic episodes every night was evidence I had not been dealing properly with my fears and anxieties. I had ignored them for the most part, hoping they would go away on their own. My mind, however, kept sending the signals until eventually my body got involved—a wake-up call of heart palpitations, shortness of breath, and uncontrollable quivering is quite impossible to ignore. I was unsure of what I needed to do to stop the episodes. The stress and lack of sleep was definitely beginning to take its toll on me emotionally and physically. I needed to find a way to cope with these nightly events or eliminate them all together. One early morning after being awakened by another episode, I got out of bed, found a paper and pen, and began to write. I made a list of all of my worst fears—losing a family member, being left completely alone in life, making a fool of myself, being let down by friends, etc. Then I came up with a list of twelve key questions to ask myself about each individual fear I had listed. By approaching my fears in this methodical way, I was able to see that most of my fears were irrational and would most likely never occur.

TWELVE KEY QUESTIONS:

- Has this happened in the past?
- If it has, did the pain of the event kill me?
- How did I survive the pain?
- What did I learn from the event?
- Would I survive the event if it happened again?
- Is it realistic to think that I can avoid this pain forever?
- Is there anything I can do to prevent it?
- What is the cost of preventing the pain?
- Is it worth the cost?
- Am I willing to do the work to overcome or avoid this pain?
- What does that work look like?
- Who can I ask for support?

Once I could see that many of my fears were irrational, I no longer needed to spend time worrying about them. It was not probable I would ever be left completely alone without any family or friends. I also realized I could avoid some of the things I feared, but the cost for avoiding that pain was too high. For example, I could prevent being let down by friends by not having any friends. But the pain of not having friends is far worse than taking the chance that one of them may let me down at some point. I was willing to take the risk of getting hurt by a friend because the thought of having no friends at all was a much scarier proposition to me. I could also see that many of my fears were merely thoughts of past painful events I did not want to experience again, as well as imagined future events that I wished to avoid. One recurring fear I'd had since Jaron's suicide attempt was that he would eventually try again and succeed in taking his own life. My fear of losing my son was so intense that for a period of time I insisted on calling him several times a day to make sure he was okay. I also made a rule that no matter where he was or what he was doing, he had to answer his phone immediately and assure me of his well-being. This strategy obviously did not provide me with the comfort and assurance I was hoping for, as was evidenced by my nightly panic episodes. It wasn't until Jaron sat me down and explained to me how my overwhelming fear was stifling him that I began to try to let go of my fear. Jaron assured me he would never again attempt to end his life, and I needed to trust him to make the right decisions and to take care of himself. I had to let it go.

Letting go of fear and anxiety is not as easy as it may sound. If living in a constant state of worry and fear has become a habit, it can be extremely difficult to overcome. However, long-term health effects such as high blood pressure, irritable bowel, tension headaches, insomnia, digestive problems, and an increased risk of heart attack and stroke are possible and even likely if the anxiety is not addressed. By using the twelve key questions to address each of my fears, I was able to begin the recovery process and let go of my anxiety. I also came up with a plan to handle the panic episodes when they occurred. If I awoke in the middle of the night in a state of panic and fear, I would take a few deep breaths, then repeat in my mind something like: "Everyone is okay. Michael and Corinne are at home sleeping. Jaron is in his bed sleeping. Devin is downstairs asleep. David is next to me sleeping. Everyone is okay. I am okay." While repeating this, I would try to imagine my voice sounding tranquil, calm, and sleepy. I would even imagine myself yawning and feeling very relaxed.

This sort of self-hypnosis is a trick I learned when I read Paul McKenna's book, "I Can Make You Sleep." Paul teaches that changing the tone of the internal voice evokes a relaxation response in the body. Once my body began to relax, I would offer a silent prayer or make a mental gratitude list until I was able to go back to sleep. If at that point I was still unable to sleep, I surmised I was awake because God had an important message for me, and I waited for that message to present itself. Most of the time, one or a combination of all of these methods was sufficient to diffuse the panic episode. Eventually, the episodes became less and less frequent and now most of the time I am able to sleep through the night without any problems.

The biggest factor in overcoming my anxiety episodes was deciding that I could. It was up to me. No one could make my fears go away but me. They were my creation, after all, and it was therefore my responsibility to kick them to the curb. Once I made the decision to face my fears instead of ignore them and came up with a plan to address them, the healing began.

> *"Perfectionism is self-abuse of the highest order."*
> *– Anne Wilson Schaef*

Let Go of Perfection

I used to have an idea of what my perfect life would be like. When David and I were first married and talked about having children, we knew what kind of family we would have. We would have a girl first, followed by a boy or two, and then maybe another little girl would come along and complete our perfectly balanced and happy little family. The boys would be basketball players and the girls would be beauty queens. We would all go to church together every Sunday and our children would sit reverently and listen intently to what was being taught. There would never be any fighting or quarreling, only kind words spoken and loving gestures given. After our children had grown up and become doctors and presidents of companies, they would all live close by and we would see them and our grandchildren every day. Our lives would be wonderfully happy and nothing bad or unpleasant would ever happen to burst our perfect little bubble.

Okay, so maybe we weren't quite that naïve, but in many ways I think we were. At least, I was. Looking back now, I can see that the family I had created in my head was not real or even possible. I had an idea of what my "perfect family" would be like, and I tried, I really did, to make it a reality. But trying to make a real family into a perfect one is an impossible task because perfection is simply not obtainable. Nothing can exist in a state of perfection permanently. In the beauty of a blooming flower or the magnificence of a sunset, there is a temporary moment of perfection, but it quickly fades away. We are not made to reach perfection in this life, and if we are able to in the next life, I think it will be a long, long process.

One of my favorite poets is Robert Frost, and I love his poem "Nothing Gold Can Stay". By comparing human life to the cycles of nature, Frost reminds us that even the best moments are fleeting, and we should enjoy them while they last. Reflecting on the words to this poem brought to mind memories of my children when they were small. They were so full of energy, excitement, joy, and love. I regretted the fact that I had often been so preoccupied with having things "just so" that I had wasted many opportunities to enjoy this magical time with my boys. I wished I had taken more time to play and talk with my sons instead of insisting they clean their rooms or do their chores. I should have colored more, laughed more, read more, played cars more, and relaxed more as a young mother. I should have worried less about whether their hair was combed or their clothes were clean and folded and put away. I should have asked them earlier about what activities they wanted to pursue, instead of assuming I already knew. I remember signing up our boys for community soccer leagues and junior basketball teams. It was what everyone we knew who had children did, so that's what we did. Our oldest son loved playing sports and enjoyed these activities. But my middle and youngest sons were not very interested in playing. In fact, they hated it. Many tears were shed and countless practices were endured before my husband and I realized we were making our sons miserable. We had a vision of what our family life was supposed to be, and we were working to make it happen. We were busy trying to create our ideal life. Once we let go of our plan for them and let them choose for themselves the activities they wanted to participate in, they and we were much happier.

In so many areas of my life, I had longed for perfection. I wanted a perfect family, a perfect body, and a perfect home. And, to some extent, I think there is merit in striving for the best and not settling for less than we deserve. However, when taken to the extreme, perfectionism can become a chain around our necks, a club with which we beat ourselves over the head. Expecting my body to be some ideal size or shape or number had caused me to hate myself for years on end. Expecting my children to behave only how I wanted them to, and do only what I thought they should do, was stifling them and robbing them of their agency. Expecting my home to look like the cover of a magazine at all times was driving me crazy and was not realistic in the least. We did live there, after all. I needed to find a way to release my need for perfection, and embrace the beautiful imperfection of the process of living. Could I learn to appreciate the small moments of perfection while they were here, and then let them go, knowing that at some point they may return again? Could I admit that perfection was just an illusion, and that, instead, I could strive to enjoy the process of learning, growing, and improving?

Edwin Bliss said, *"The pursuit of excellence is gratifying and healthy. The pursuit of perfection is frustrating, neurotic, and a terrible waste of time."* I wanted to stop wasting time and energy striving for the so-called perfect life, but first I needed to know why I was doing this. Why did I feel driven to seek a "perfect" life, body, home, and family? What was it that caused me to think I could possibly control all aspects and details of my own and my family's lives? I thought of my childhood and the home I grew up in. My mother had a rigid cleaning schedule. Her house was, and still is, immaculate, right down to the sparkling clean sinks, the dust-free furniture, and the freshly vacuumed carpets. In fact, it was our family joke that if you got up in the middle of the night to use the bathroom, when you came back, your bed would be made. It was possible that growing up in a clean and structured environment had instilled in me the desire to create the same environment in my own home. I did enjoy having a well kept home, much like the one I grew up in. But, even so, I felt I had taken it to the extreme, making it a higher priority than it should be and creating an atmosphere of tension in our home instead of the warm, loving environment I had envisioned.

In her book, "He Did Deliver Me From Bondage, author Colleen C. Harrison teaches us we all have some kind of addiction we turn to when we feel overwhelmed by life. For some, it is addiction to food or alcohol. For others, drugs or sex fill the void. As I read the book, I began to realize that my perfectionism was not necessarily a result of my upbringing—it was a desperate attempt to gain control. I wanted to be in charge. I wanted my life the way I wanted it. I wanted my body to be a certain weight and shape. I wanted my home to be perfectly clean and orderly at all times. And, worst of all, I wanted my family to live up to my expectations of perfection instead of letting them just enjoy life and be themselves. I had set such impossibly high standards that no one, not even me, could live up to them. Instead of feeling accomplished, powerful or capable, I felt frustrated, inadequate, and anxious. My efforts to have a perfect little family were creating a divide where I was striving for unity. I was setting us all up for failure by trying to achieve the impossible. Logically, I knew I didn't really have control over everything that happened in life. There is no way to prevent every accident, foresee every tragedy, and avoid every heartache. But logic doesn't always enter into our minds when we are engaging in addictive behaviors. And, for me, that is what perfectionism had become—an addiction.

The problem with addictive behaviors is that they don't actually solve our problems. They only give us temporary reprieve or escape from the problem without offering any long-term solutions. By striving for perfection, I was satisfying the part of my brain that was addicted to control, but continually falling short left me feeling empty and defeated. It was a never-ending cycle. As it turns out, I was not the only one who was dealing with this challenge. A study by Mental Health America based on data from 2002 to 2006 revealed Utah to be the most depressed state, and other studies found that toxic perfectionism was a major cause of depression among LDS women. Many other studies have also linked the personality trait of perfectionism to poor overall health, migraine headaches, chronic pain, asthma, high anxiety and stress levels, depression, and an increased risk of death. As an LDS woman living in

Utah, I was one in a group of thousands or even tens of thousands of women with unrealistic expectations and standards. Crisis counselors in some emergency rooms in Utah have even noted an increase of LDS women suffering from depressive symptoms and anxiety related problems on Sunday evenings and following church meetings. I don't happen to believe that the church is imposing standards of perfection on their members, although expectations for righteousness are very high. I think that a great number of women of my faith, and many other belief structures as well, are imposing those expectations upon themselves. In Matthew 5:48, Jesus commands his disciples to, *"Be ye therefore perfect, even as your Father which is in heaven is perfect."* The Greek origin of the word *perfect* means to be whole or complete. How different would our approach be if we worked towards being whole and complete instead of striving for the impossible goal of perfection?

I don't know if I ever would have been able to break the cycle of perfectionist behavior if I had not been blessed with the amazing children that I have. Thankfully, the walls of my imaginary perfect home and family life came tumbling down a few years ago when my then eighteen-year-old son, Jaron, came out to me. Around the same time, my youngest son, Devin, who was twelve, began to come to me with concerns that he was a bad person because he thought he might be gay. To say I was shocked would not be accurate, because I believe on some level, I did know both of my youngest sons were gay. But, I had been living in my imaginary bubble for so long, it took me by surprise when they both came to me, separately, to share with me their true feelings about their identities. Here I was, busily planning my sons' futures: serve an LDS mission, go to college, marry a nice girl in the temple, have children, and live close enough for me to see them and my grandchildren regularly. Meanwhile, they had struggled for years with the idea they were somehow flawed or bad because of who they were.

I was not devastated by these revelations or ashamed of my sons in any way. I love and accept them for exactly who they are and I admire them for their courage and fortitude. However, I was ashamed of myself for not being able to see beyond my vision of the "perfect family" for such a very long time. While Jaron never blamed me, I felt an enormous amount of guilt that he felt he had to pretend to be something he wasn't in order to be accepted in our community and by his family. And although Devin came forward to me much earlier in his life, I felt I somehow could have offered more support to him than I had. Unfortunately, at the very time he was struggling with his emerging sexual identity, I was dealing with Jaron's attempt at suicide, and most of my attention was focused on helping him recover and on helping the rest of our family heal. But, now that my imaginary bubble had burst, I was able to see clearly what a wonderful family I had right in front of me. I no longer needed to try to form a picture-perfect home and family life because that type of family didn't even exist. No one has a perfect family, but I believe we are all given the family that is perfect for us—the family that we need in order to learn to become our best selves. I could finally see how incredibly blessed I had been all along.

Once I realized I was addicted to trying to control and perfect everything, I was able to begin the process of surrendering. I repeated to myself each day, "God is in control of my life, and I only control how I respond to what happens." This simple affirmation helped me to see I did not have to take responsibility for every single event or person in my life; I only had to worry about how I personally handled whatever occurred. It came as a tremendous relief to know it was not my job to make everything okay and picture-perfect. I also practiced giving myself a break and leaving things undone from time to time. I experimented with things like leaving the unfolded laundry in a pile on my bed, not planning a weekly menu, or not balancing the checkbook, and do you know what happened? Nothing. Nobody died or suffered. I didn't go into cardiac arrest or burst an artery. Eventually, the things that needed to get done were done, even if it was not exactly perfect. I started to let myself be vulnerable in ways I never had dared before. I even posted a no make-up selfie on social media! Letting others see me in a less-than-ideal state was freeing and exhilarating; and honestly, there was only one person who even noticed I wasn't wearing any make-up in the picture.

I began to notice the beautiful imperfections in nature and my surroundings—two strawberries in my garden that had fused together to create a delightfully lumpy single work of art. The gnarly, twisted branches of the cedar tree in my front yard that created an interesting silhouette. The oddly shaped black spots on my little dog's back that could only be seen when I gave her a bath. I even noticed the beautiful imperfection of famous people with large noses, facial scars, or gapped teeth-their imperfections were what made them attractive, recognizable, and real.

Once my imaginary world came crashing down around me and the walls were finally gone, I could see and appreciate things as they really were. I could see failure as an opportunity to learn rather than seeing it as proof of my inadequacy. I began to realize I could fall short, make a mess, screw things up, and make a fool of myself and still be just fine. I could admit nobody gets it right one hundred percent of the time. I could celebrate small victories and stay in the moment instead of constantly thinking ahead to some future perfect moment that never arrived. Surrendering is not about giving up. It's about giving up the need for control. It's about putting your trust in God and knowing he is the one driving the bus, and you are just along for the crazy, exciting, breathtaking ride.

"When you ask God into your life, you think he or she is going to come into your psychic house, look around, and see that you just need a new floor or better furniture and that everything needs

just a little cleaning – and so you go along for the first 6 months thinking how nice life is now that God is there. Then you look out the window one day and see that there's a wrecking ball outside. It turns out that God actually thinks your whole foundation is shot and you're going to have to start over from scratch."
-- Marianne Williamson

Let Go of Doubt

I have had a few wrecking ball moments in my life, some of which I have shared in this book. I think those moments come in all of our lives when we have to choose whether to accept God's will or stubbornly keep insisting we have things our way. We may say we want to grow and learn, but, when it comes right down to it, we are afraid because we know there will be growing pains involved. We may proclaim we want to change, progress, and become better, but we are full of doubts that we will ever really be more than what we are. We often allow our limiting beliefs about ourselves and about life to hold us back from being all we were meant to be, all that God intends for us to be. I have wanted to write a book for most of my life, but I had doubts that I would ever be able to actually do it, and those doubts held me back from even trying for decades. Some psychologists estimate as much as ninety percent of self-talk is negative. Everyone has doubts, fears, negative thoughts and limiting beliefs. But, the fact that negative self-talk exists, doesn't mean we have to buy into it. We can overcome negative self-talk and let go of doubts by following our inner wisdom, finding someone who believes in us, asking empowering questions, and taking a leap of faith.

Deep inside each of us is a reservoir of stillness and light. This is the part of ourselves that knows what is right for us. Many call it conscience, intuition, or spirit; I like to call it "inner wisdom." No matter what term you use to describe it, our inner wisdom will never lead us down a wrong path. Years ago, my husband and I decided to build a new home. We searched for almost a year for the "perfect" lot to build on (that should have been my first clue). Finally, David found a lot he was really excited about and wanted to make an offer on. I did not feel right about the lot, but I couldn't give an exact reason why. The neighborhood was nice and the neighbors were friendly, but something about it just didn't feel right to me. Being tired of the yearlong hunt for a place to build, I ignored my inner wisdom and agreed we should make the offer, never telling my husband of my reservations. Needless to say, we did not have a pleasant building experience. Our dream home turned out to be a nightmare. We spent a year working with an unethical builder to create a home we didn't really want in a place that was not right for us. We sold the home five months after moving in. If I had listened to my inner wisdom instead of just going along with what felt right to someone else, we may have had a different experience. However, I do believe we learned a great deal from that experience and we eventually ended up in the home we now live in, which we feel is exactly where we need to be. Since then, I have always tried to follow my inner wisdom, even when I don't have a good reason or it doesn't make sense.

Finding someone who believes in you and in your ability to succeed is a huge factor in overcoming self-doubt. I heard a song once that tells the story of an old man who wants to pass his driver's test, but his son refuses to give him the keys. With tears streaming down his face, the old man turns away and just gives up, never to drive a car again. The line that brings tears to my eyes every time is, "Tell me, how would you feel? You'd probably give up too, if nobody believed in you." *(Harley Allen, If Nobody Believed in You, 2004)* Having an ally, someone who sees your potential and believes in your abilities, will do more than almost anything else to help you overcome your doubts and move toward your dreams. When I was thinking of going back to school to become a health coach, my friend, Brandon, knowing of my efforts to live a healthy lifestyle, came to me asking for some health advice. I told him of my plans to possibly sign up for the training, and also shared with him my reservations and the many reasons why the timing might not be right. His enthusiasm and support were one of the main reasons I made the decision to take the leap and register for the classes, even though David and I were also helping two of our sons pay for college at the same time. Pursuing my goal didn't make much sense financially, but we were able to manage the expenses, and I will always be grateful for the friends and family members who encouraged and believed in me.

Asking empowering questions can be a great way to overcome doubt. When we reframe a situation in order to see the possibilities instead of the limitations, we can move past our fears, doubts, and insecurities and bring forth the success and growth that we desire. In her book, "Supreme Influence", Niurka gives us the formula for crafting questions that will propel us toward our goals and aspirations.

1. Begin the question with *how, what* or *who*. These three words set the stage for understanding and success. Some examples are, *"What can I do right now to accomplish _____?"* or *"What would I do if I knew I could not fail?"*

2. State the question in the affirmative. This will keep you flowing in the direction you want to go, toward your vision. Focus on what you want, not on what you don't want. For example, the question, *"How can I not be such a procrastinator?",* reinforces old patterns, whereas, *"How can I be more focused on accomplishing my goals?",* is more affirmative and results-oriented.

3. Build momentum with words like *right now, while,* and *even more*. Using this language implies you are already moving toward the goal and causes your brain to begin finding the answer immediately.

Some good examples are: *"How can I tune into the inner peace within me right now?"* and, *"How can I be even more lean, healthy and fit right now while savoring foods I love?"*

Niurka teaches us that by creating empowering questions, we open ourselves to limitless possibilities and potential. She writes: *"Your life reflects the quality of the questions you ask. When you elevate your questions, you elevate your entire experience of reality."*

One of my favorite scriptures is found in Luke 1:37: *"For with God nothing shall be impossible."* When we invite God into our lives and surrender to His will, we take a leap of faith. And, we may indeed, wake up one day and see His wrecking ball hovering right outside our window. However, we can be assured that nothing is too hard for Him. We may feel hopeless and beyond help. We may be discouraged and lost. We may not be able to see how we can ever overcome the many obstacles along our path. But, He can. He knows each one of us individually and is waiting to give us the guidance and wisdom that we need in order to live our very best lives. When my journey to wellness began at age thirty, I was scared I would never regain the vibrancy, energy, and health I had once enjoyed. But, I soon learned that by gradually implementing spiritual habits into my daily life, I could feel better not only on an emotional level but physically as well. I learned my body did matter to God, that He cared about me and wanted to help me heal. He wanted me to experience a fullness of joy in this amazing body that He gave to me. I was created in His image, so I had no doubt that He could show me how to care for my physical body in a spiritual way. All I had to do was ask, and I received.

CREATE THE HABITS

Let Go of Fear:

1. Make a list of your deepest, darkest fears and answer the twelve key questions for each one. If a fear is irrational, let it go, realizing it could never really happen. If it is a rational fear, come up with a plan for how you will handle it, if the event you fear ever comes to pass.
2. When fears and worries keep you awake at night, try Paul McKenna's self-hypnosis method by changing the tone of your internal voice from stressed and anxious to calm, relaxed, and sleepy.
3. Remember that fears are merely signals from your brain that a problem needs to be addressed. Use prayer, gratitude, and stillness to find answers about how to best approach resolving those issues.

Let Go of Perfection:

1. Instead of striving to have a perfect body, home, family, or life, practice enjoying the beautiful imperfection of these things just as they are. Set an alarm on your cell phone to chime at the same time every day. When you hear the chime, use it as a reminder to appreciate the beauty of the moment you are in.

2. Spend a few hours watching TV. Make a list of all the people you see who have unusual features such as scars, gapped teeth, or large ears. Appreciate these people, and yourself, for their beautiful imperfections.

3. Take a walk in nature and observe the unusual and peculiar sights. Note how Mother Nature creates beauty out of chaos. Make a list of ten beautifully imperfect things you see.

4. Practice leaving a few things undone every now and then. Leave the laundry unfolded for a day, ignore the phone, or skip going to the gym and notice what happens. Pretend you are a scientist conducting an experiment and make note of your findings.

Let Go of Doubt:

1. When making decisions, always listen to your inner wisdom, even if it doesn't make sense to you at the time. Trust your gut and move forward in faith.
2. Talk with friends and family members about your goals and aspirations. Seek out those who are positive, supportive, and encouraging and feed off their enthusiasm.
3. Use Niurka's 3-Step formula below to create empowering questions that will set you up for success in reaching your goals.

   - Begin the question with *how, what*, or *who.*
   - State the question in the affirmative
   - Build momentum with words like *right now, while*, and *even more.*

4. Take a leap of faith and turn your life over to God. Recognize that as your creator, He will give you the guidance you need in order to care for your body, mind, and spirit in the very best ways possible.

Affirmations:

- God is in control of my life; I only control how I respond to what happens.
- I embrace the process of perfecting rather than the illusion of perfection.

- I am at peace with all things exactly as they are right now.
- I appreciate the small moments of perfection while they are here and let them go, knowing they will eventually return again.
- I recognize and appreciate the beautiful imperfections in nature, in others, and in myself.
- I am able to overcome all doubts and fears because, with God, nothing shall be impossible.

Use this space to write your own surrender habits and affirmations:

Sources

Habit #1: Gratitude

Gordon B. Hinckley, *Standing for Something: 10 Neglected Virtues that will Heal our Hearts and Homes,* (New York: Times Books, Random House, 2000), 91-92.

Rhonda Byrne, *The Magic,* (New York: Atria Books, Simon & Schuster, 2012), 150.

Deepak Chopra, Debbie Ford, & Marianne Williamson, *The Shadow Effect: Illuminating the Hidden Power of Your True Self,* (New York, Harper Collins, 2010), 86, 95, 156.

Habit #2: Learning

Csikszentmihalyi, Mihaly, *Flow: The Psychology of Optimal Experience.* (New York, NY: Harper and Row, 1990).

Joseph B. Wirthlin, "Come What May and Love it," *Ensign,* November 2008.

Habit #3: Stillness

Eckhart Tolle, *A New Earth: Awakening to Your Life's Purpose,* (New York, Plume, 2006), 21-22, 255.

Michael A. Singer, *The Untethered Soul,* (Oakland, Noetic Books, 2007), 94-95.

Joshua Rosenthal, *Integrative Nutrition,* (New York, Greenleaf Book Group, 2007).

Meditation, accessed on en.wikipedia.org/wiki/Meditation.

Andrew Weil, M.D., *Natural Health, Natural Medicine: The Complete Guide to Wellness and Self-Care for Optimum Health,* (New York, Houghton Mifflin, 2004) 127-129.

Habit #4: Humility

Movie, *The Help,* (Touchstone Pictures, 2011). Based on the book *The Help* by Kathryn Stockett, (Penguin Books, 2009).

Habit #5: Surrender

Paul McKenna, *I Can Make You Sleep,* (New York, Sterling Publishing, 2009), 97.

Robert Frost, *Nothing Gold Can Stay,* (Yale Review, October 1923).

Colleen C. Harrison, *He Did Deliver Me From Bondage,* (Hyrum, Windhaven Publishing, 2002).

James Thalman, "Utah Leads the Nation in Rates of Depression," (Deseret Morning News, Nov. 29, 2007). Accessed on www.deseretnews.com/article/695231614.

Harley Allen, *If Nobody Believed in You,* Joe Nichols, Revelation CD. (Universal South, 2004).

Niurka, *Supreme Influence: Change your Life with the Power of the Language You Use,* (New York, Crown Publishing, 2013) 182-187.

Final Thoughts

Writing this book has been a wonderful journey and a dream come true for me. I wholeheartedly believe every word I have shared with you, even though my attempt to live up to and apply them in my own life is an ongoing process. It is my hope that one day we can all see ourselves as we really are—amazing, courageous, cherished children of a loving God. I look forward to the day when we are all a little kinder to one another and to ourselves, the day when we acknowledge the precious gifts that we all have been given. Our bodies are one of those many gifts, and I believe that nurturing them to the best of our ability is a sacred stewardship that we have been given. My mission as a health coach is to support as many people as possible in learning to do just that.

I have so much more I would love to share with you, so please feel free to contact me through my website: www.lindabarneyhealthcoach.com

My blog: www.pathtowellness-linda.blogspot.com

or email: lbbarney25@gmail.com